Aanjikiing / Changing Worlds
An Anishinaabe Traditional Funeral

Lee Obizaan Staples

AANJIKIING / CHANGING WORLDS

An Anishinaabe Traditional Funeral

Lee Obizaan Staples
Chato Ombishkebines Gonzalez

MINNESOTA
HISTORICAL
SOCIETY PRESS

With the editorial assistance of Michael Migizi Sullivan Sr. and John D. Nichols.

Note: No royalties are paid to the authors or editors.

Originally published as Memoir 22, Algonquian and Iroquoian Linguistics (Winnipeg, Manitoba: 2015).

Minnesota Historical Society Press edition 2023

mnhspress.org

The Minnesota Historical Society Press is a member of the Association of University Presses.

Manufactured in the United States of America

10 9 8 7 6 5 4 3 2 1

♾ The paper used in this publication meets the minimum requirements of the American National Standard for Information Sciences—Permanence for Printed Library Materials, ANSI Z39.48-1984.

International Standard Book Number
ISBN: 978-1-68134-279-5 (paper)

Library of Congress Control Number: 2023935541

Library and Archives Canada Cataloguing in Publication

Obizaan Staples, Lee, 1945– , author
    Aanjikiing = Changing worlds : an Anishinaabe traditional funeral / Lee Obizaan Staples & Chato Ombishkebines Gonzalez.

(Algonquian and Iroquoian linguistics, memoir ; 22)
Text in Ojibwe and English.
ISBN 978-0-921064-22-0 (paperback)

    1. Ojibwa language—Texts. 2. Ojibwa Indians—Funeral customs and rites. 3. Ojibwa Indians—Social life and customs. 4. Ojibwa Indians—Religion. I. Ombishkebines Gonzalez, Chato, 1980– , author. II. Algonquian and Iroquoian Linguistics, issuing body. III. Obizaan Staples, Lee, 1945– . Aanjikiing. IV. Obizaan Staples, Lee, 1945– . Aanjikiing. English. V. Title. VI. Title: Changing worlds. VII. Series: Memoir (Algonquian and Iroquoian Linguistics) ; 22

PM851.O25 2015   497'.333   C2015-907516-5

Table of Contents

GE-NAADAMAAGOYAN DA-MIKAMAN ENDAZHINJIGAADEG OMAA

TABLE OF CONTENTS

Lee Obizaan Staples and Chato Ombishkebines Gonzalez

PREFACE

Those of us fortunate enough to know Lee *Obizaan* Staples know of the sacrifice he has made for his fellow *Anishinaabe* people. Since the very first funeral he conducted almost twenty years ago, *Obizaan* has answered the call of the tobacco that always seems to find him and never seems to cease. By accepting the tobacco in 1995 to conduct his own brother's funeral, *Obizaan* gave away his own life and freedom to serve his *Anishinaabe* people. If you have ever had the pleasure to talk with him, you've most likely heard him say how he had just done "back-to-back" funerals. From his home community at *Aazhoomog* near Hinckley, Minnesota, to places as far as Sault Ste. Marie, Ontario, *Obizaan* has traveled the breadth of *Anishinaabewakiing* following the path that the tobacco leads. Most of us who will read this book and rely on its contents into the future have had our own relatives sent home by *Obizaan* to the place that we have been given as *Anishinaabe*.

Aside from his work with funerals, *Obizaan* is also a drum-keeper in our sacred Big Drum society. Twice a year he puts on one of the grandest drum ceremonies in all of Ojibwe country with his co-owner Larry *Amik* Smallwood. People come from far and wide to support him and hear his teachings of the drum. In addition to his own semi-annual drum dance ceremony, *Obizaan* regularly attends and is regularly relied upon at dances at Lac Courte Oreilles, Wisconsin and has been as far west as White Earth, Minnesota and as far east as Lac du Flambeau, Wisconsin to support his fellow drum members in those communities.

In the summertime, from mid-May to early September, *Obizaan* spends his time in a wigwam in the woods on the Mille Lacs reservation in central Minnesota conducting the ancient *Midewiwin* ceremonies that he learned from his elders a generation ago. All summer long, *Obizaan* helps initiate people into the sacred *Midewiwin*. Every once in a while during the summer months, his lodge ceremonies will be delayed due to his having to "do some funerals." Many of our relatives who were once struggling with the various challenges of life and have found counsel and direction from *Obizaan* would attribute the fact that they are alive and well today to their time spent with him in his ceremonies.

Obizaan is in high demand in other ceremonies that he regularly conducts. I recently heard him say that he has over 400 namesakes on whom he has bestowed their *Anishinaabe* spirit names. Almost every evening he is on the go; whether it be a memorial feast for someone who has passed on, a naming ceremony, or an offering of food and tobacco for someone in need, *Obizaan* works tirelessly to ensure that the teachings that we have been given as *Anishinaabe* people continue into the future for the sake of our relatives yet to come. As modest and humble as he is, *Obizaan* is indeed an international spiritual leader and a principal authority on the spiritual life of the *Anishinaabe* people.

It should be stated that some might view the publishing of this book as inappropriate or even offensive. For a long time, as a result of our historic and often tragic experience, our ways were kept secret and our ceremonies were out-of-sight. As a result, some considered the recording of our ceremonies and even of our language in written form to be taboo. This was not much of an issue a generation ago. Elders at that time had individuals younger than them such as *Obizaan* who were fluent in the language and versed in the spiritual teachings of the *Anishinaabe* people. Times are different today. With language shift complete in many communities and near completion in all others, we simply do not have the time, the language ability or the spiritual depth to learn these teachings in the traditional oral-only manner of yesteryear.

As I write this preface, I can count on my hands all the individuals that I know personally who are capable and qualified to conduct traditional *Anishinaabe* funerals. Some of our communities have lost all of their elders who were once responsible for sending their relatives home. These communities rely heavily upon the work of *Obizaan*. As he states in the Introduction:

> *The reason why I am having this written down is that in the future there are going to be fewer people who know how to send the Anishinaabe spirit to that other world. This is my thinking: Why should I be stingy with what I have been taught. I do not own it. This teaching belongs to and was gifted to the Anishinaabe people. There will be no merit if I try to hold on to all this for selfish reasons and take it all with me when I pass on. It is meant to be shared so there are others in the future who can carry on these teachings.*

As with most aspects of traditional ways and spiritual teachings, there are variations to the teachings and some may find portions of the following pages different from the versions they have come to know. What appears before you is **Obizaan's** version, a version he received from **his** elders. All too often we conceptualize our spiritual understanding in a binary manner— what is the "right way" as opposed to the "wrong way." Critics of this volume should keep in mind that such opinions show disrespect for *Obizaan* and his work, along with the countless number of elders before him who have simply offered what they had been taught by the ones before them. An accusation of anything being "wrong" or "incomplete" is an accusation directed toward individuals who have forgotten more than most of us will ever know. I encourage any such critic to match the contribution that *Obizaan* has provided, not only in the form of this book, but in the depth and degree to which he has served his people. Critics are urged to consider who they will rely upon to send them home or, perhaps more relevant, who will send their children and grandchildren to them when their time arrives. Most of us will never hold a candle to the work of *Obizaan*.

In addition to *Obizaan's* immeasurable contributions, this work would never have been carried out without Chato *Ombishkebines* Gonzalez's commitment and perseverance in not only this particular project, but in his holistic approach to language learning and ceremony. *Ombishkebines* was personally selected by *Obizaan* to be the one to carry these teachings forward into the future. Chato deserves a great deal of recognition for stepping up to the call of the tobacco as well, while many have shied away from such responsibilities. *Obizaan* would also like the reader to be mindful that this book is not intended to be a "leisurely read," but a guide to those who have been chosen to carry on this work. As Chato himself explains in the Acknowledgements, young men before him that paved the way in their language learning have inspired him to learn Ojibwe, the most crucial tool of our spiritual realm. Chato's own work is sure to inspire others to pursue our language and the beautiful way of life we have been given as *Anishinaabe*.

The book that appears before you is the result of many work sessions, multiple drafts and revisions, and discussions of words and grammatical forms. Chato *Ombishkebines* Gonzalez collected the contents of the book via dictation from *Obizaan*. After establishing each paragraph, the two would then work out the English that appears on the corresponding pages. Though their sessions were obviously extremely productive, *Obizaan* often remarks on how many times he wanted to fire Chato for driving him crazy with his persistent and never-ending questions.

Upon the completion of each chapter, they would provide me with a copy for review. My role was basically to serve as a spell-checker, ensuring that their versions complied with the spelling and punctuation conventions of the double-vowel orthography established by Charles Fiero and modified slightly by John Nichols. Spelling conventions and the presentation of entries in the glossary follow those of Nichols & Nyholm's *Concise Dictionary of Minnesota Ojibwe* (1995) and the online Ojibwe People's Dictionary.

After making my comments and posing questions pertaining to certain vocabulary and grammatical issues, Chato worked through each chapter with *Obizaan* discussing the forms in question. After *Obizaan* had an opportunity to consider each issue and revise as he saw fit, the drafts of each chapter were then sent to John Nichols for his review. Nichols then provided his own questions and suggestions regarding the presentation of the manuscript, which were brought back to *Obizaan* for consideration. Since we served as mere reviewers of the textual form, we had no audio to consult during our review and essentially had no way of knowing whether certain issues we called into question were actually accurate orthographic representations of something *Obizaan* said or, perhaps more commonly, Chato's own transcription shortcomings or errors. The reader is advised to keep in mind that the issues that had arisen out of this review process were mainly questions pertaining to our own linguistic interests as well as to our lack of understanding as linguists regarding certain nuances of Ojibwe grammar.

Perhaps more important than our extensive external review process is the fact that *Obizaan* himself had multiple opportunities to revise and craft the written representation of his language. A major and unavoidable consequence of this lengthy editing and revision process is that the final draft that is presented to you does not necessarily match the way *Obizaan* speaks Ojibwe. Speaking a very colloquial style of Ojibwe, *Obizaan* will be the first to tell you, and many of his language students have heard him say it, "I chop all kinds of stuff up when I talk." As a result, a number of features of Ojibwe morphology which native speakers are notorious for omitting are represented here in the written form. These include personal prefixes (*ni-*, *gi-*, *o-*), short vowels (*a-*, *i-*, *o-*) that are often deleted word-initially, short vowel syncopation (not nearly as prolific as that occuring in Odawa), and the morpho-phonological form and extent of Initial Vowel Change. For the most part, those omissions have been restored and regularized here in agreement with *Obizaan's* preferences regarding the written representation.

It is also important to note that the corresponding English approximations have not received much attention over the course of this review process, serving mainly as our guide for navigating through the Ojibwe. Rather than hashing out a literal or even loose direct translation, *Obizaan* simply provided an English explanation of each Ojibwe paragraph. As the reader will notice, *Obizaan* does a much better job at providing a more eloquent and sophisticated English explanation than others might provide in translation. Any errors found in either language are solely the fault of us as reviewers and editors, not at all of *Obizaan*.

While linguists might like to see a detailed account of a vocal performance, L2 speakers and teachers of Ojibwe are sure to appreciate the presentation of what might be considered a "proper" or more "formal" style of Ojibwe literature. All too often, our claims made regarding our understanding of grammar and typology has been based on impromptu "shoot from the hip" vocal performances. With the exception of a few published works, our native-speaking contributors are seldom given an opportunity to revise and craft their contributions. Speakers (including *Obizaan*) and students of Ojibwe will agree that the version presented in this book represents a formal and proper form of Ojibwe prose. Those interested in studying and analyzing phonetic and (morpho-)phonological phenomena should contact the authors directly as they have established an extensive audio library. In addition to this volume, they have compiled a number of published stories, articles, and forthcoming books.

In conclusion, as language death falls upon many tribes in North America and indigenous peoples across the world, some Ojibwe communities in Minnesota and Wisconsin have begun large-scale language revitalization efforts. With the success seen in the Ojibwe immersion schools, the Ojibwe language very well might make it to another generation and beyond in those communities. The generations after *Obizaan* will surely appreciate this work the most. Long after the critics have gone on, most likely having taken their teachings with them, the work of *Obizaan* and the teachings that he has so graciously shared will live on. *Geget igo chi-gizhewaadizi aw Chi-Obizaan. Miigwech nagadamawiyaang!*

Michael *Migizi* Sullivan Sr.
Odaawaa-zaaga'iganing
7 Gichi-manidoo-giizis 2015

NIWII-MIIGWECHIWITAAGOZ

Nimiigwechiwi'aag ingiw Manidoog gii-shawenimaawaad odanishinaabemiwaan gii-miinigoowiziyang o'ow akeyaa da-ni-izhichigeyang naa biinish wenda-onaajiwang gaa-miinigoowiziyang ge-ni-izhaayang gegoo izhiwebiziyang.

Nimiigwechiwi'aa Chi-Obizaan gii-shawenimid apii gii-kagwaadagitooyaan gii-pi-naazikawid gii-pi-wiindamawid wii-naadamawid da-ni-gikendamaan ge-ni-izhichigeyaan weweni da-ni-bimiwidooyaan i'iw nibimaadiziwin. Mii dash gaa-izhichiged a'aw akiwenzii gii-anoozhid da-babaamidaabii'iwetamawag babaa-naadamawaad inow Anishinaaben ganoodamawaad anooj i'iw akeyaa ani-asemaakenid.

Mii dash i'iw gomaapii gaa-izhi-gagaanzomid a'aw Obizaan da-biminizha'amaan da-ni-gikendamaan gidinwewininaan. Mii dash gaa-izhichiged, nigii-kikinoo'amaag iniw ikidowinan imaa ani-dazhinjigaadeg menidoowaadak, mii dash imaa gii-maajitaad gii-kikinoo'amawid i'iw gaagiigidowin ani-aabajichigaadeg maajaa'iwed awiya. Mii iw gikinoonowin i'iw niizhosagoons miinawaa ishwaaswi ezhi-wiindang a'aw wayaabishikiiwed apii weweni gaa-maajitaad gii-kikinoo'amawid i'iw Ojibwemowin.

Mii dash gaye apii gii-moonendamaan, mii i'iw ge-naadamaagoyaan weweni da-ni-izhi-bimaadiziyaan, aaniish naa mii i'iw akeyaa gaa-inendaagoziyang anishinaabewiyang da-ni-izhi-bimiwidooyang i'iw bimaadiziyang. Geget ingii-ayaangwaamitoon gii-piminizha'amaan da-gikendamaan i'iw Ojibwemowin. Ginwenzh igo omaa ingii-nanaamadab ani-agindamaan miinawaa ani-bizindamaan ge-naadamaagod da-ni-gikendang da-ojibwemod awiya. Gaawiin debinaak ingii-izhichigesiin, ishke dash noongom gaawiin igo aapiji indaa-ni-

ACKNOWLEDGEMENTS

I want to express my gratitude to the Manidoog for all the compassion they have for their Anishinaabe in giving us this ceremony and for giving us that beautiful place to go to when anything happens to us.

I want to express my gratitude to Lee Staples for taking pity on me when I was going through hard times, and for approaching me and telling me he was willing to help me to learn what I needed to do to live a good life. What that old man did was hire me to drive for him when he went out and about talking for the Anishinaabe's tobacco when they had their various feasts.

Then after a while he began to encourage me to learn how to speak Ojibwe. What he had done was teach me the vocabulary used in the ceremonies that he conducted, and then he started to teach me the actual talks that went with doing an Anishinaabe funeral. It was in 2008 that he began to teach me to speak Ojibwe.

It was then that I realized that it was all these teachings that would help me live a good life, after all this was the way of life we were given by the Manidoog to live. I really took it seriously and worked hard and diligently to learn our language. I sat for long hours reading Ojibwe texts and listening to recordings of Ojibwe speakers to help me learn how to speak Ojibwe. I did not approach all this half-heartedly, and because of that I am able to understand the Ojibwe spoken to me, and am seldom stumped by the words spoken to me.

wawaanimigosiin awiya ojibwemotawid.

Ishke gaye ani-babaa-wiijiiwag a'aw akiwenzii, mii gaye imaa wendinamaan ani-wiikwajitooyaan ani-gagwe-gikendamaan aaniin igo akeyaa eni-izhichiged a'aw Anishinaabe ani-asemaaked ani-manidoowichiged. Ishke dash mii iw ani-maajiikamigaag o'ow aki waa-ni-izhichigeyaan niwii-kikinoo'amawaag niniijaanisag da-ni-apiitendamowaad gaa-izhi-ina'oonwewiziyang anishinaabewiyang da-ni-bimiwidoowaad ge-wiinawaa aazhita da-ni-gikinoo'amawaawaad oniijaanisiwaan azhigwa ani-ayaawaawaad.

Niwii-miigwechiwi'aag a'aw Biidwewekwe naa Mandaamin gii-onaabamiwaad da-wiidanokiimag a'aw akiwenzii. Ogii-mikaanaawaa i'iw akeyaa ge-izhi-diba'amaagooyaan da-ni-aabiji-wiijiiwag naa gaye da-naadamawag a'aw Obizaan. Gii-minochigewag a'aw Biidwewekwe naa Mandaamin gii-inaakonigewaad i'iw akeyaa da-ni-izhiwebak da-ni-gashki'ewiziyaan ani-bimiwidooyaan da-ni-izhichigeyaan a'aw akiwenzii eni-izhichiged ani-ganoodamawaad inow wiiji-anishinaabeman. Gaawiin igo aapiji giniigaaniiminaang da-ayaasiiwag ge-ni-gikendangig gaagiigidowin ani-aabajichigaadeg imaa maajaa'iweng miinawaa anooj i'iw akeyaa eni-izhichiged a'aw Anishinaabe ani-asemaaked. Gaawiin aapiji ayaasiiwag noongom i'iw akeyaa ezhi-gikinoo'amawinjig da-ni-gikendamowaad da-ni-bimiwidoowaad o'ow gaagiigidowin ayaabijichigaadeg ani-maajaa'iweng biinish gaye ani-manidoowichigeng. Geget dash gii-wenda-minochigewag a'aw Biidewewekwe naa Mandaamin.

Nebowa igo ayaawag gechi-aya'aawijig gaa-naadamawijig gii-kikinoo'amawiwaad biinish gaye gii-aanikanootamawiwaad iniw ikidowinan, mii dash a'aw miigwechiwi'ag a'aw

As I traveled with the old man, I began to learn the various ceremonies that Anishinaabe people were given. What I plan to do in the future is to teach my children what I have learned and to appreciate the way that we have been given by the Manidoog to carry ourselves, and in return for them to go on and teach their children, when they have their children.

I also want to express my appreciation to Joyce Shingobe, former Commissioner of Education, and Melanie Benjamin, Chief Executive of the Mille Lacs Band of Ojibwe, for selecting me to work with Obizaan. They found a way to hire me to constantly travel with Obizaan to help him. Joyce and Melanie did a good thing in their decision to create a position so that I am able to travel with the old man as he continues to go about and speak for the Anishinaabe as they do their ceremonies. In our future there will not be many who will know the talk that goes with doing an Anishinaabe funeral, and also for the various other Anishinaabe ceremonies. There are very few if any who are being taught how to conduct an Anishinaabe funeral or any of our other ceremonies. This is why I say that it was a good decision made by Joyce and Melanie to support what we are doing.

There are many elders who have helped me along the way and have taught me to speak Ojibwe and translated words that I did not understand. Some of these elders are Larry Smallwood,

Amikogaabaw, Manidoo-bizhiki, Waabishkibines, Zaagajiw, Jiingwewegaabawiban, Gaagebiikwe, Niigaanigaabawiikweban, Waasebiikwe, Zhaangweshiiban, Ogimaakwe. Ayaadogenag wenenimagig, gaawiin onjida indizhichigesiin. Mii igo weweni ani-miigwechiwi'agwaa gaye wiinawaa.

Miinawaa niwii-miigwechiwi'aag a'aw Migizi miinawaa a'aw Biidaanakwad. Ishke ginwenzh gii-ni-nanaamidabiwidogenag gii-ni-baabiitawi-agindamowaad i'iw indoozhibii'igan nanda-waabandamowaad miinawaa nanaa'isidoowaad gii-wanibii'igeyaan.

Ayaawag igaye gaa-wenda-ombi'ijig ingiw nawaj eni-oshki-bimaadizijig azhigwa gaa-ojibwemowaad, geget gii-wawiingeziwag. Mii dash i'iw gaa-inendamaan ganabaj igo gaye niin indaa-gashki'ewiz da-ni-gikendamaan gidinwewininaan. Mii dash a'aw Waawaakeyaash miinawaa Waagosh maamaw-wayeshkad gaa-noondawagig ojibwemowaad. Mii omaa gaa-onjikaamagak gii-wenda-anokiitamaan wii-gikendamaan Ojibwemowin. Mii iw wayeshkad gaa-noondawagig, ishke dash noongom nebowa ayaawag beminizha'angig i'iw Ojibwemowin, geget ninaadamaagon noondawagwaa ojibwemowaad gaye wiinawaa.

Niwii-miigwechiwi'aag gaye ingiw besho enawemagig wenjida a'aw nishiime Waasegiizhigookwe miinawaa owiij'ayaawaaganan Niizhoogwaneb, mii ingiw genawenimaajig niniijaanisan megwaa gikinoo'amaagoziyaan naa gaye a'aw akiwenzii babaa-wiijiiwag. Booch gaye niwii-miigwechiwi'aa nimaamaa Bimise-jiigibiigookwe, naa gaye nookomisiban Biidaabanookweban, biinish gaye nizhishenyag bemiwidoojig gidizhitwaawininaan. Mii ingiw gaa-

Doug Sam, Joe Nayquonabe, Ralph Pewaush, Benny Rogers, Misko binayshi, Mary Jane Frog, Anna Gibbs, Rose Tainter, and Lillian Rice. There may be some that I may have forgotten; I am not deliberately leaving them out. I am expressing my gratitude to all of them also.

I also want to express my gratitude to Michael Sullivan, Professor at the College of Saint Scholastica, and John Nichols, Professor at the University of Minnesota-Twin Cities. They sat for long hours reading our materials over and over again, editing them, and correcting me in the errors that they may have found.

There are also those second-language speakers that motivated me as I heard them speak Ojibwe fluently. That is when I thought and began to realize that I was also capable of learning how to speak our language as they have done. It was Keller Paap and Anton Treuer that I first heard speak Ojibwe fluently. It was as a result of hearing them that I was inspired to work hard to learn our language. They were just the first ones that inspired me, but today there are many who are pursuing the language. To hear them speak has also motivated me.

I also want to thank my family, especially my younger sister Rosie Gonzalez and her husband Raymond Hart Jr. They are the ones who took care of my children while I was in school and when I was out traveling with Obizaan. I also have to thank my mother Cynthia Tudjen and my late grandmother Saxon St. Germaine, along with my uncles who carried on our ceremonies. They also are the ones who taught me how to live my life in a good way and as Anishinaabe should.

kikinoo'amawijig gaye wiinawaa i'iw akeyaa ge-izhi-
bimiwidooyaan i'iw nibimaadiziwin.

Giwii-miigwechiwi'ininim gaye giinawaa egindameg omaa
wezhibii'igaadeg waabanda'iweyeg apiitendameg gaa-izhi-
miinigoowiziyang anishinaabewiyang.

Ombishkebines

I also want to thank you for reading this book and showing your interest and appreciation for our teachings as Anishinaabe.

Chato Ombishkebines Gonzalez

Aanjikiing / Changing Worlds

1 GAA-ONJIKAAMAGAK O'OW

Obizaan indizhinikaaz. Mii omaa Gaa-zhiigwanaabikokaag endaashaan. Mii-ko omaa moozhag ani-naadamaageyaan imaa Misi-zaaga'iganiing ishkoniganing ani-ganoodamawag a'aw Anishinaabe ani-asemaaked.

Gaawiin nigii-aanoodizisiin miinawaa gaawiin nigii-piminizha'anziin i'iw da-maajaa'iweyaan.

Mii o'ow gaa-izhiwebiziyaan. Nigii-wani'aa a'aw nisayenh. Ishke dash ingiw dedebinawe besho enawemagig, gaawiin nigii-pi-wiij'ayaawaasiig. Bakaan ingoji iwidi nigii-nitaawigi'igoo. Mii a'aw akiwenziiyiban nimishoomeyiban miinawaa a'aw ninoshenyiban gaa-nitaawigi'ijig. Mii ingiw gaa-odedeyiwiyaan miinawaa gaa-omaamaayiwiyaan. Mii ingiw wenjida gaa-saagi'agig.

Ishke dash owapii gii-inaakonigewaad waa-ni-izhichigeng wii-maajaa'ind a'aw nisayenh, gaawiin imaa nigii-ayaasiin. Mii iw bijiinag owapii i'iw giizhigadinig waa-na'inigaazod a'aw nisayenh gii-pi-dagoshinaan imaa.

Ishke dash inow owiiwan ogii-onaabamaan inow ge-maajaa'iwenijin. Ishke dash azhigwa waa-ni-maajitaang mii a'aw gii-pazigwiid a'aw gaa-onaabamind da-maajaa'iwed. Mii dash o'ow gaa-ikidod, "Gaawiin indaa-maajaa'iwesiin onzaam noomaya inendaagwad gii-wani'ag a'aw nindede."

Mii dash i'iw gii-kaagwiinawendamawaad awenenan ge-maajaa'igojin nisayenh. Mii dash owapii gii-pi-gagwejimigooyaan da-maajaa'iweyaan. Mii dash imaa gii-nakwetamaan da-izhichigeyaan i'iw akeyaa, aaniish naa gaawiin awiya gii-ayaasiin imaa ge-nitaa-maajaa'iwed.

2

1 INTRODUCTION

My name is Obizaan. I live in Hinckley, Minnesota. I do most of my work on the Mille Lacs Reservation talking for the Anishinaabe and the tobacco they are offering.

I did not desire nor did I pursue the work of sending people off through traditional funerals.

This is what happened to me. My older brother had passed on. I was not raised with my biological brothers and sisters. I was raised elsewhere. My mother's sister and her husband raised me. These are the ones I considered my mother and my father. They are the ones I was especially close to.

When funeral arrangements were made for my older brother, I was not there. It was not until the actual day of the burial that I had arrived.

It was his wife who selected someone to do the funeral. At the start of the funeral the individual who was selected to do the funeral stood up to say, "I cannot do the funeral because I recently lost my father."

So as a result they did not know who was going to do the funeral. It was then that they approached me and asked me to do the funeral. I had to say yes, since there was nobody there that knew how to do a traditional funeral.

Mii dash owapii gii-ni-maajitaad a'aw Anishinaabe gii-pi-
naazikawid asemaan ininamawid da-maajaa'iweyaan. Zanagad
geget i'iw maajaa'iweng. Nigagiibaadenimaa a'aw Anishinaabe
mesawendang miinawaa wenda-aanoodizid wii-biminizha'ang
wii-maajaa'iwed. Giishpin i'iw enendaagoziyan da-
maajaa'iweyan, oda-ni-mikaanaawaa ingiw Manidoog i'iw
akeyaa da-ni-maajitaayan da-ni-bimiwidooyan da-ni-
naadamaageyan. Eshkam da-ni-bangiiwagiziwag netaa-
maajaa'iwejig. Booch ingiw Manidoog da-onaabamaawaad
inow ge-inenimaawaajin i'iw akeyaa da-ni-naadamaagenid.

Mii iw wenji-ayaamaan o'ow da-ni-ozhibii'igaadeg. Ishke
eshkam da-ni-bangiiwagizi ge-nitaa-maajaa'iwed. Mii o'ow
akeyaa enendamaan: Aaniin dash ge-onji-zazaagitooyaambaan
i'iw gaa-izhi-gikinoo'amaagoowiziyaan. Gaawiin niin
indibendanziin. Mii a'aw Anishinaabe gaa-miinigoowizid o'ow
giigidowin. Gaawiin gegoo da-inaabadasinoon ani-
ayaangwaami-minjiminamaan i'iw gaa-izhi-
gikinoo'amaagooyaan da-ni-maajiidooyaan azhigwa gegoo eni-
izhiwebiziyaan. Maanoo da-ayaawag ge-ni-bimiwidoojig i'iw
akeyaa gaa-izhi-miinigoowiziyang anishinaabewiyang.
Miinawaa gaye asemaa wiisiniwin ingii-atoomin weweni da-
doodawindwaa ingiw Manidoog gaa-pi-miinaajig iniw
Anishinaaben o'ow akeyaa ge-izhichigenid.

Mii omaa da-ni-dazhindamaan gaa-onjikaamagak i'iw-sa
akeyaa gaa-izhi-gikinoo'amaagoowiziyaan-sa i'iw
maajaa'iwewin. Mii a'aw akiwenziiyiban gaa-nitaawigi'id, mii
a'aw Ogimaawabiban gaa-izhinikaazod. Gii-maajaa'iwe iko
a'aw akiwenziiyiban. Ishke dash a'aw mindimooyenyiban gaa-
nitaawigi'id gaye Nazhikewigaabawiikwe gii-izhinikaazo. Nigii-
paa-wiijiiwaa iko a'aw mindimooyenyiban gii-o-bizindawangid
a'aw akiwenziiyiban gii-maajaa'iwed.

It was since then that the Anishinaabe began to approach me with their tobacco asking me to do these funerals. It is definitely difficult sending the spirit of our people off through this ceremony. I find it foolish when I hear of Anishinaabe who aggressively pursue the desire to do funerals. If it is meant for you to do funerals, the Manidoog will find a way for you to begin helping in this way. If it is meant to be, it will happen; do not try to make it happen. In the future there will be fewer people who will know how to do these funerals. In time the Manidoog will select those who are meant to help in this way.

The reason why I am having this written down is that in the future there are going to be fewer people who know how to send the Anishinaabe spirit to that other world. This is my thinking: Why should I be stingy with what I have been taught. I do not own it. This teaching belongs to and was gifted to the Anishinaabe people. There will be no merit if I try to hold on to all this for my own benefit, for selfish reasons, or take them to my grave. It is meant to be shared so there are others in the future who can carry on these teachings. We also put tobacco and food in respect to the Manidoog who gave these teachings to the Anishinaabe.

I will now talk about where all the teachings on doing these funerals came from. The old man that raised me, John Benjamin, did these funerals. The old lady that raised me, her name was Sophia Churchill-Benjamin. I would travel with that old lady and we would listen to that old man when he did funerals.

Ishke dash mii o'ow maamaw-zanagak ani-gaagiigidod awiya o'ow-sa maajaa'iweng. Nebowa iko a'aw akiwenziiyiban ogii-ni-wanendaan ani-dazhinjigaadeg maajaa'ind awiya. Mii dash i'iw azhigwa gaa-pi-giiweyaang gaa-kiizhiitaad, mii imaa gii-nanaamadabiyaang gii-ni-waawiindamawind a'aw akiwenziiyiban gaa-waniiked imaa gii-ni-gaagiigidod. Mii-go gegapii a'aw mindimooyenyiban gii-ni-ozhibii'ang i'iw gaagiigidowin da-naadamaagod a'aw akiwenziiyiban gegoo aapiji da-ni-waniikesig imaa gaa-achigaadeg i'iw gaagiigidowining. Mii dash gaye niin wenjikaamagak mikwendamaan-sa ezhising i'iw gaagiigidowin.

Azhigwa gaa-moonendamaan a'aw Anishinaabe wii-naazikawid da-maajaa'iweyaan, mii a'aw nizhishenyiban Mizhakwadoban gaa-asemaakawag nawaj da-ni-gikinoo'amawid i'iw gaagiigidowin.

Mii gaye gaa-kikinoo'amawid a'aw nizigosiban Nazhike-awaasangoban. Gii-maajaa'iwe iko a'aw mindimooyenyiban gii-ayaasinig imaa ge-ni-gaagiigidonipanen.

Mii gaye a'aw gaa-naadamawid a'aw awedi bezhig nizigosiban Amikogaabawiikweyiban. Mii iwidi gii-wiij'ayaawag a'aw mindimooyenyiban. Naano-biboon imaa nigii-wiij'ayaawaa iwapii gii-pi-azhegiiweyaan iwidi chi-oodenang gii-paa-ayaayaan. Geget nigii-kagaanzomig a'aw mindimooyenyiban da-ni-bimiwidooyaan noongom ezhichigeyaan.

Mii gaye weweni gaa-pizindawag gii-kaagiigidod imaa maajaa'iwed. Mii dash a'aw akiwenziiyiban Niibaa-giizhikoban. Weweni nigii-asemaakawaa a'aw akiwenziiyiban.

This is the most difficult talk to do — telling the spirit what he will see as he journeys to the other world. Because of this, the old man would forget a lot that goes into the talk for these funerals. When we would get home after he had finished a funeral, we would sit down and we would cover the things that he had forgot in his talk. Eventually that old lady wrote down the talk to help the old man not to forget what he was to say. It is from there that I remember how the talk goes with these funerals.

When I realized that the Anishinaabe would be approaching me to do funerals, I went to my uncle Albert Churchill and gave him tobacco to give me additional teachings in doing funerals.

The other person who taught me was my aunt Mary Churchill-Benjamin. She had done funerals when there was no one available to do them.

The other who gave me help on this was my aunt Julie Shingobe. I stayed with her for five years after I came back from living in the Twin Cities. She is the one who really encouraged me to do what I am doing today.

The other one I listened to carefully as he did funerals was Archie Mosay. I had given tobacco to that old man to learn from him.

Ishke dash gaye gidaa-manaaji'aawaa a'aw gaa-o-miinind inow asemaan da-bi-maajaa'iwed imaa endanakiiyeg. Gidaa-gagwejimaawaa weweni aaniin i'iw akeyaa ge-izhi-ozhiitaayeg wii-maajaa'aad inow gidinawemaaganiwaan. Ishke ishkweyaang gii-onjikaamagadini i'iw akeyaa eni-izhichiged ani-maajaa'iwed. Ogii-gikinoo'amaagoon inow akiwenziiyibanen naa gaye inow mindimooyenyibanen iwidi wenjibaad. Gaawiin odaa-aanjitoosiin i'iw akeyaa gaa-izhi-gikinoo'amawind da-maajaa'iwed. Gego dash ani-wiindamawaakegon a'aw mayaajaa'iwed da-ni-aanjitood i'iw akeyaa gaa-izhi-gikinoo'amaagoowizid da-ni-wiindamaweg, "Mii-ko o'ow akeyaa ezhichigeyaang omaa maajaa'iweng." Ishke aano-go ani-gikendamaan maajaa'iwewin, gaawiin indaa-wiindamawaasiin mayaajaa'iwed da-ni-aanjitood imaa ezhichiged wiin maajaa'iwed.

Geget a'aw Anishinaabe ogii-pi-inigaa'igoon inow wayaabishkiiwen. Ishke a'aw chi-mookomaan ogii-aanawenimaan inow bemaadizinijin inow bakaan enaanzozhenijin biinish igo gaye ingiw bakaan enendaagozinijin da-ni-izhi-bimaadiziwaad. Mii imaa gaa-onjikaamagadinig a'aw Anishinaabe gii-aanooji'igod inow wayaabishkiiwen da-ni-debweyendanzig da-ni-bimiwidoosig i'iw akeyaa inow Manidoon gaa-inenimigod da-ni-izhi-bimaadizid biinish gaye da-ni-ikowebinang i'iw gaa-miinigod inow Manidoon da-ni-inwed.

Ishke mewinzha iwidi gii-onjikaamagadini gii-ni-waawiindamaagoowizid a'aw Anishinaabe da-ni-goopadeninindizod biinish gaye geyaabi imaa ani-ayaamagadini ani-waawiindamaagoowizid da-ni-aanawenindizod anishinaabewid wenjida imaa mezinaateseg genawaabandamang noongom. Mii-go gegapii a'aw Anishinaabe geget igo ani-debwetang gaa-inind naa-go geyaabi enind goopadizid, mii-go imaa biinjina ani-debwetang.

Be respectful and ask the one selected what he wants done to prepare for the funeral of your relative. His teachings on how to do a funeral came from the old men and the old ladies of the past that resided in his community. He cannot change the way he has been taught so be respectful of that. Do not ask him to make changes or conform by telling him that, "This is the way it is done in our community." Even though I know how to do these funerals I would not tell the one doing the funeral to make changes to conform to the way that I have been taught.

The Anishinaabe have really been treated badly by the white man. The white man regarded those of a different color and those who were given a different way of life as being inferior. As a result the white man went after the Anishinaabe to not believe in or to carry on the way of life given to the Anishinaabe to live and to abandon the language given to the Anishinaabe by the Manidoog.

It started way back when the Anishinaabe were told they were inferior and that message still comes across through the TV sets we watch. Eventually the Anishinaabe believed what they were being told how they were inferior and this is what they are still being told today and they began to believe that within.

Ishke niwii-ni-dazhimaa a'aw abinoojiinh enigaachigaazod imaa endazhi-ganawenjigaazod, maagizhaa gaye inow ogitiziiman maagizhaa gaye netaawigi'igojin odinigaa'igoon. Mii imaa apane noondang, "Geget gigoopadiz". Ishke moozhag ezhi-wiindamawind a'aw abinoojiinh iw akeyaa, mii-go gegapii izhi-debweyendang goopadizid. Ishke dash nebowa a'aw Anishinaabe, mii-go dibishkoo gaa-izhiwebizid, mii imaa biinjina goopadenindizod dibishkoo-go gaawiin omaa biinjina apiitenindizosiin miinawaa gaawiin zaagi'idizosiin biinjina. Ishke dash gaawiin onanaa'isidoosiin imaa enenindizod imaa biinjina. Ishke dash ingiw nebowa mii imaa epa'iwewaad maagizhaa gaye nanaandawi'iwewaad gemaa gaye midewi'iwewaad miinawaa anooj igo akeyaa baa-manidookaazowaad. Mii imaa enendamawaad owiiji-anishinaabemiwaan da-ni-mamiikwaamigowaad miinawaa da-ni-apiitenimigowaad. Ishke dash wenji-aanoodiziwaad wii-ni-izhichigewaad i'iw akeyaa, mii imaa wenjikaamagadinig biinjina goopadenindizowaad. Gaawiin i'iw akeyaa da-inaabadasinoon i'iw gaa-miinigoowiziyang. Ishke ayaawag ingiw mayaajaa'iwejig, gaawiin dash weweni ogikendanziinaawaa i'iw da-ojibwemowaad naa-go wawaaj igo midewi'iwewaad.

Giishpin gii-pi-gagwejimigooyan da-maajaa'iweyan miinawaa gikendanziwan i'iw gaagiigidowin nawaj wenipanad "Gaawiin" da-ikidoyan. Gego gikendamookaazoken. Gidaa-inigaa'aa ge-maajaa'ind biinish gaye inow odinawemaaganan. Nibiingeyenimaa a'aw Anishinaabe ani-nakwetang ani-anoonind i'iw da-ganoodamaaged misawaa-go gikendanzig.

Gizhiiwen imaa ani-gaagiigidoyan ani-maajaa'iweyan. Mii eta-go akeyaa a'aw Anishinaabe ge-ni-izhi-gikendang i'iw gaagiigidowin. Ani-gizhiiwewaad ingiw mayaajaa'iwejig

I want to talk about the child that is being abused by their parents or foster parents. They constantly hear the message that they are worthless. When a child hears that constantly, he eventually begins to believe he is worthless. This is what happened to a lot of the Anishinaabe, they had believed those negative messages and internalized the idea that they are worthless; they do not have high self-esteem or love for themselves within. This way of thinking has not been addressed or changed. As a result of this a lot of Anishinaabe try to become medicine men, try to run Midewiwin lodges, and attempt various ceremonies to raise their own self-esteem. And as a result of all that they expect their fellow Anishinaabe to brag them up, put them on a pedestal, and to elevate their status in their mind to make them feel good about themselves. This is why they are so determined to do those ceremonies. All this stems from them feeling worthless inside. These ceremonies should not be used in this way. Now we have those who do funerals and run our Midewiwin lodges even though they do not know the language.

If you are asked to do a funeral and you do not know how, it is much easier to just say no. Do not act like you know how. You could hurt the one being sent off and also his or her relatives. It blows my mind to hear of Anishinaabe who agree and accept the job of talking for the Anishinaabe's tobacco when they do not know how.

When you do a funeral speak loudly. This is the only way Anishinaabe will learn how the talk goes. When those who are doing the funeral speak loudly, they are heard properly. Some people doing funerals cannot even be heard when they speak.

weweni da-noondawindwaa. Mii-go aanind gaawiin debitawaasiiwag ani-gaagiigidowaad.

Ishke dash booch weweni da-nagadenimad waa-ni-ganoonad apane, mii-go dibishkoo ingiw Manidoog. Mii iw gaa-naadamaagoyaan. Mii iw endaso-gigizhebawagak, mii imaa gii-nanaamadabiyaan ingoji-go aabita-diba'igan. Mii-ko imaa gii-kanoonagwaa ingiw Manidoog bebezhig gii-ininamawagwaa inow indasemaaman. Ginwenzh igo ingii-izhichige i'iw akeyaa. Gomaapii-go gaa-izhi-odisiwaad ingiw Manidoog gii-pi-zhawenimiwaad. Mii-go gaye imaa gii-ni-moozhitooyaan i'iw menidoowaadak wenda-mashkawaamagadinig gegabiwaad ingiw Manidoog. Ishke dash mii iw nayaadamaagoyaan ani-maajaa'iweyaan gayat gii-ni-nagadenimagwaa ingiw Manidoog geganoonagig. Ishke izhichigesig i'iw akeyaa a'aw geganoodamaaged, mii iw akeyaa ge-initaagozid dibishkoo-go odagindaan i'iw ezhi-gaagiigidod. Mii-go ge-izhi-gikendamowaad ingiw bezindookig, dibishkoo-go gaawiin gegoo imaa biinjina ayaamagasinoon ani-gaagiigidoyan.

Mii imaa okobii'igaazowaad aanind ingiw Manidoog gaa-kanoonagig endaso-gigizhebaawagak ingiw Manidoog a'aw Anishinaabe epenimod:

- Manidoo Naagaanizid
- Miinawaa Owiiji-manidooman
- Manidoo omaa Akiing
- Miinawaa Owiiji-manidooman
- Manidoog iwidi Waabanong
- Manidoo iwidi Zhaawanong
- Manidoo iwidi Ningaabii'anong
- Manidoo iwidi Giiwedinong
- Binesiwag
- Manidoo omaa Misi-zaaga'iganing

You have to form a relationship with the person who you are talking to, and the same applies to the Manidoog. That is what helped me. Every morning I would sit for a half hour or so. I would offer my tobacco to each Manidoo one by one. I did this for a long time. After a while the Manidoog came to me and took pity on me. Each time I felt the spiritual energy and the power the Manidoog sit with. This is what helps me when I am doing a funeral since I already have built a relationship with the Manidoog that I am speaking to. If the one who is talking for the tobacco does not do this, you can hear it when they talk. It sounds like they are reading a script. The people who are listening will know and it will be as if there is no depth to what you are talking about.

Here is a listing of some of the Manidoog that I spoke to each morning that Anishinaabe rely on for help:

- Leader of the Manidoog
- Also, those who are with him/her
- Manidoo here on Earth
- Also, those who are with him/her
- Manidoog that sit in the East
- Manidoo that sits in the South
- Manidoo that sits in the West
- Manidoo that sits in the North
- Thunder-Beings
- Manidoo in Mille Lacs Lake

- Manidoo omaa Waabashkikiing
- Awesiinyag
- Bebiiwaabaminaagozijig Awesiinyag
- Mendidojig Awesiinyag
- Memiigwanaajig
- Mitigwaabiiwininiwag
- Manidoog omaa Nibiikaang
- Ziibiing; Zaaga'iganiing
- Wenabozho
- Miinawaa ogookomisan, Gookomisakiinaan
- Gakina Manidoog
- Chi-oshkaabewis
- Giganaan (Dibiki-giizis)

Anooj Manidoog:

- Nazhike-awaasang
- Naawi-giizhik
- Anangoog
- Gaa-biboonike
- Memengwesiwag (Manidoo-gwiiwizensag)
- Bagwajiwinini
- Nabaanaabe
- Gimishoomisinaanig, Bayaabiiwaabikishingig

Gidaa-wii-mikwendaan, mii inow ojichaagwan a'aw waa-ni-aanjikiid ge-ni-ganoonad ani-gaagiigidoyan. Ishke mii imaa ani-apiichitaang ge-ni-gweki-manidoowid. Mii-go gaye imaa da-ni-naadamaagoowiziyan ani-ganoonad inow ojichaagwan ani-dazhiikawad a'aw gidasemaam ezhi-gikinoo'amaageyaan omaa.

- Manidoo in the Swamp near East Lake
- Animals
- Little Animals
- Big Animals
- Birds
- Trees
- The Manidoog in the Water
- Lakes; Rivers
- The Manidoo Who Once Lived among Us
- Also his grandmother
- All the Manidoog[1]
- The Sun
- The Moon[2]

Various other Manidoo:

- The Star that Shines Alone (Evening Star)
- Center of the Sky
- The Stars
- The Manidoo in the Snow
- The Little People in the Woods
- The Big Man in the Woods
- Mermaid
- Our grandfathers, the Rocks on this Earth

Remember it is the spirit of the individual that is about to leave that you will be addressing. The spirit will change into a Manidoo as we go along in this ceremony. This will also help you when you speak to the spirit of the deceased if you use your tobacco as I have instructed.

1 Add this to cover the ones you may have forgotten.
2 She is the one who will correct any mistakes or anything left out.

Bakaan izhichigem miinawaa bakaan izhi-gaagiigido awiya ani-mide-maajaa'iwed, ani-maajaa'ind a'aw abinoojiiyens, ani-maajaa'ind a'aw abinoojiinh gaa-pabaamibatood omaa akiing, biinish gaye zaagi-maajaa'iweng. Maagizhaa ingoding giniigaaniiminaang nindaa-dazhindaanan inow.

Mii-ko imaa abiitawind awiya ani-dazhinjigaadenig gaa-onjikaamagadini gii-miinigoowizid a'aw Anishinaabe ge-ni-izhaad gegoo izhiwebizid. Ishke gayat nigii-ozhibii'aamin gaa-inaajimind a'aw Wenabozho miinawaa inow odoozhiman, apii gii-miinigoowizid a'aw Anishinaabe ge-ni-izhaad gegoo izhiwebizid.

Bakaan dash noongom ayaamagad eni-inaajimoyaan, mii dash a'aw Amik gaa-gikinoo'amawid. Mii inow gaa-inootawaajin inow akiwenziiyibanen, Gete-bwaaniban gii-izhinikaazo. Mii dash a'aw akiwenziiyiban gaa-ikidod "Azhigwa a'aw Wenabozho gii-kikina'amawaad inow odoozhiman da-bi-biindigesinig imaa gii-taawaad. Mii iw gaa-inaad, «Gego omaa bi-biindigeken, mii ow gayat gii-mawiyaan, mamiiziwe ingiw Manidoog ingii-noondaagoog. Indawaas igo ani-ozhitoon i'iw miikanens ge-ni-izhaad a'aw gidanishinaabeminaan gegoo ani-izhiwebizid.»"

Gaawiin niwanishkwe'igosiin imaa bakaan izhigiizhweng; ayaa a'aw Manidoo ge-ni-nanaa'isidood giishpin imaa ani-waniwebinigeng.

Gaawiin daa-ginigisijigaadesinoon ow akeyaa a'aw Anishinaabe gaa-izhi-miinigoowizid miinawaa a'aw wayaabishkiiwed ezhichiged anama'e-maajaa'aad awiya. Biindigajigaadeg i'iw chi-mookomaan ezhichiged imaa Anishinaabe-maajaa'iweng, mii-go imaa da-ni-bitaakoshkangiban a'aw eni-maajaa'ind. Gaawiin iwidi da-ni-dagoshimoonosiin ezhaanid a'aw gidanishinaabeminaanan.

16

There is a different way of doing things and a different way to talk when doing a Midewiwin funeral, infant funeral, toddler funeral and funerals where the water drum is brought in to use even though the deceased was not Mide. Maybe at a later date I could cover these.

It is at the wake where the history of all this is talked about and how the Anishinaabe were given a place to go when something happened to them. We have already written down the story about Wenabozho and his nephew giving the Anishinaabe a place to go when anything happens to them.

I now tell a different version of this story nowadays, which Larry Smallwood taught me. He learned this from Jimmy Jackson. That old man said when Wenabozho told his nephew's spirit not to come into their dwelling, he told him, "Do not come in, I have already begun my crying and the Manidoog everywhere have heard me. Just go on and make that path where our Anishinaabe can go when something happens to them."

I am not bothered by this different way of talking, because there is that Manidoo that will correct it if an error is made.

Do not mix the way that we have been taught to do funerals with the white man's way of doing funerals. If we bring the white man's teachings into the way we do our funerals a barrier would be created preventing the spirit of the deceased from reaching that place where our people go.

Aaningodinong inow aazhaweyaatigoong agokajigaadeg inow waabigwaniinsan aana-wii-pi-biindigajigaadewanoon imaa endanakamigak. Booch daa-wii-mamigaadewanoon inow. Wawaaj igo gaye aanind iko obiizikaanaawaan naabikawaaganan imaa agoojing a'aw aazhaweyaatig. Niwiindamawaanaanig da-giizikamowaad i'iw naabikawaagan maagizhaa gaye da-gaanaawaad inow aazhaweyaatigoon baazikawaawaajin.

Gaawiin i'iw bakaan daa-izhichigesiin awiya. Ishke imaa ani-dagosijigaadenig i'iw bekaanak, dibishkoo-go imaa ani-wiindamawaawag ingiw Manidoog aanawendamang gaa-izhi-miinigoowiziyang da-izhichigeng maajaa'iweng. Nebowa a'aw Anishinaabe odaana-wii-gikinawaabamaan inow wayaabishkiiwen ezhichigenid danakamigizinid o'ow akeyaa. Gego a'aw Anishinaabe daa-izhichigesiin wiin i'iw akeyaa.

Eshkam nebowa a'aw Anishinaabe omisawendaan da-ni-jaagizigaadenig owiiyaw azhigwa gegoo ani-izhiwebizid. Maagizhaa gaye ogosaan inow manidoonsan da-ni-amogod azhigwa imaa dabazhish ani-na'inigaazod. Mii-go gaye gwetamowaad gibishkaagod inendang awiya imaa wenda-agaasatemagadinig ayaad, mii iw gaye mekwendamowaad.

Ishke gaawiin i'iw odaa-babaamendanziin a'aw Anishinaabe. Gaawiin wiin imaa anaamakamig da-ayaasiin; mii eta-go i'iw owiiyaw imaa ge-ayaamagadinig imaa anaamakamig. Azhigwa ani-maajaa'ind, mii iw wiin iwidi da-ni-bima'adood i'iw miikanens gaa-miinigoowiziyang da-maada'adooyang gegoo ani-izhiwebiziyang.

Mii iw gaye a'aw Anishinaabe ge-ni-waabandang isa da-wenjised jaagizigaazod. Gaawiin gaye i'iw odaa-babaamendanziin a'aw Anishinaabe. Zhooniyaa omaa abi inow ishkoniganan da-diba'igaadenig na'inind awiya miinawaa gaye

18

Sometimes wreaths in the shape of crosses are brought in that have flowers attached onto them. The wreaths have to be removed. Sometimes those at the funeral will wear a necklace with a cross hanging on it. We ask them to remove those necklaces or hide them so the cross is not visible.

No one should deviate from the original way we are taught to do funerals. If we were to make changes or add to this ceremony itself, we are telling the Manidoog that we find what they have given us to be inadequate. Many of our Anishinaabe want to copy what the white man does at their funerals. We should not do this.

More and more Anishinaabe want to get cremated when they die. They are scared the bugs will eat them when they are buried. Maybe they have fears about being underground in a small place.

Anishinaabe should not have those fears. They will not be underground; it is only their physical body that will be under there. When they are sent off, their spirit will be traveling down that path we were given to take when we change worlds.

Anishinaabe also think it is cheaper to get burned down to a crispy critter. That should not be of a concern to the Anishinaabe. Today a lot of our reservations can cover the cost of our burials; if not, the welfare office can cover the cost.

ashangewigamigong onjikaa a'aw zhooniyaa diba'igaadenig na'inigaazod awiya.

Gaawiin gidaa-wanishkwebidoosiimin i'iw akeyaa gaa-izhi-gikinoo'amaagoowiziyang da-ningwa'igaazod awiya omaa akiing azhigwa gegoo izhiwebizid. Gimino-doodawaanaan a'aw Manidoo omaa eyaad akiing ningwa'igaazod awiya. Mii-go apane ani-asemaaked a'aw Anishinaabe mii-go apane epagizondamawaad inow Manidoon omaa akiing eyaanijin. Mii a'aw ginaadamaagonaan megwaa maa bibizhaagiiyang omaa akiing.

Mii dash imaa ani-nanaa'inigaazoyang omaa akiing, weweni diba'amawind a'aw Manidoo gaa-naadamawaad inow eshkwaa-ayaanijin megwaa maa gii-pibizhaagiinid omaa akiing. Gaawiin gidaa-gikinawaabamaasiwaanaanig ingiw wayaabishkiiwejig anooj izhichigewaad. Gegapii igo gaawiin niwii-maajaa'aasiin a'aw Anishinaabe o'ow bakaan ani-izhichiged.

Mii-ko aanind Anishinaabe ezhichiged noongom nandodang i'iw wiisiniwin da-bi- biindigajigaadenig iwidi wenjikaamagadinig inow Anishinaabe-babaamiziwinan iko imaa endazhi-jiibaakweng ashamind a'aw bemaadizid maagizhaa gaye iwidi ataagewigamigong onjikaamagadini. Gaawiin daa-izhichigesiiwag i'iw.

Ishke minochigewag ingiw besho enawendaasojig wiinawaa igo da-jiibaakwaadamawaad i'iw wiisiniwin weweni wii-ashamaawaad inow odinawemaaganiwaan waa-naganigowaajin. Wiinawaa ogikendaanaawaa wenjida gaa-minwendang gii-miijid a'aw waa-ni-maajaad. Biinish gaye mii imaa da-ni-ayaamagadinig da-ni-maamawichigewaad ingiw Anishinaabeg da-ni-biindigadoowaad ojiibaakwaaniwaan da-

We should not change the way we were taught as Anishinaabe, which is to be buried in the earth when we die. We are doing good to that Manidoo in the earth when we return our body to the earth. Every time the Anishinaabe put tobacco, that tobacco is sent to that Manidoo within the earth. He is the one that helps us while we are living on this earth.

As we are placed into the earth we are doing good to that Manidoo that helped us while we lived on this earth. We should not copy the white man and the way he does things. I am at that point where I will not do a funeral where changes are made.

Some of our Anishinaabe today want the food for their funerals to be provided by Indian organizations or one of our casinos. They should not do that.

The close relatives are doing good by doing their own cooking for their relative that is about to leave them. They are the ones that know what their relative especially liked to eat. This is an opportunity that should always be there for our Anishinaabe people, to help others in need by bringing in their cooking for these funerals. This is what we were taught as Anishinaabe, to help one another when something bad happens to our fellow ni-naadamaagewaad. Mii iw gaa-izhi-gikinoo'amaagoowiziyang da-ni-naanaadamaadiyang gegoo ani-maazhised a'aw giwiiji-anishinaabeminaan. Daa-wii-ni-aabiji-ayaamagad i'iw akeyaa. Onaadamaagonaawaa ingiw wesidaawendangig waabamaawaad inow owiiji-anishinaabemiwaan biindigadoonid i'iw wiisiniwin zhawenimigowaad.

Azhigwa ani-biindiganind a'aw waa-ni-maajaa'ind, mii iwidi ningaabii'anong ge-inikweshing a'aw waa-aanjikiid. Mii iwidi ningaabii'anong ayaamagak i'iw "Gaagige-minawaanigoziwining" eni-izhaayang azhigwa imaa gii-kaagwiinawaabaminaagoziyang omaa akiing.

Azhigwa omaa gaa-tagoshimoono'ind a'aw gaa-ishkwaa-ayaad, mii iwidi akeyaa waabanong ishkwaandeming akeyaa da-biindiganind. Mii iw enikweshing ge-ni-naaniigaaniimagadining azhigwa ani-biindiganind. Ani-giizhiitaang, mii dash iwidi ishkwaandem ningaabii'anong da-ni-zaagidinind a'aw gaa-maajaa'ind.

Mii-ko imaa gaa-tazhi-maajaa'iweng imaa gaa-taad gaa-wani'ind mii dash iwapii gii-saagidinind imaa waasechiganing azhigwa gaa-kiizhiitaang gii-maajaa'ind. Ishke iwidi bakaan da-ni-inakamigizing, gaawiin memwech imaa waasechiganing da-zaagidinaasiin.

Aaningodinong gaawiin baakaakonigaadesinoon inow jiibayi-makakoon da-ni-waabamind a'aw waa-ni-maajaad. Mii dash iko izhichigeyaang gikendamaang wii-paakaakonigaadesinok i'iw jiibayi-makak, mii imaa giizhaa ozhiitaang asigisijigaadenig i'iw ge-ni-maajiidood waa-ni-maajaad. Mii dash iwidi izhiwijigaadeg jiibewigamigong. Giizhaa dash imaa biinji-jiibayi-makak achigaadenig gakina ge-ni-bimiwidood azhigwa ani-maajaa'ind. Gaawiin dash memwech imaa da-ni-

Anishinaabe. That should continue to be there. It helps the grieving relatives when they see their fellow Anishinaabe bringing in their food and the compassion that is being shown toward them.

When the body of the deceased is brought in, the head should be placed facing the west. It is in the west where "The Land of Everlasting Happiness" is located. That is where we will go when we are no longer seen on this earth.

When the body is brought in, the casket is brought through the east door head first. When the funeral is over the casket will go out the west doorway.

When we used to have the funerals in the home of the deceased, that is when the body was taken out of the window. When the funeral is not done in the home of the deceased, it is not necessary to take the body out of the window.

Sometimes there are closed casket funerals. When we know we are doing a closed casket funeral, we collect all of the items to be put inside of the casket and take them to the funeral home. All of those items are then placed inside of the casket ahead of time, which he will take with him. Then it is not necessary to open the casket when it is brought into the funeral site.

baakaakonigaadesinoon i'iw jiibayi-makak azhigwa ani-
dagoshing iwidi waa-tazhi-maajaa'ind.

Aabiding gaye nigii-maajaa'aag gaa-tapinejig imaa gii-
chaagidenig endaawaad. Agaawaa-go gii-ishkwaakideni
owiiyawiwaan. Mii dash imaa moodensan gii-achigaadenig i'iw
minik gaa-ishkwaakiziwaad biinjayi'ii imaa jiibayi-
makakoonsing gii-achigaazowaad. Azhigwa gaa-ni-
ozhiitaayaang imaa wii-atooyaang iko i'iw bemiwidood a'aw
Anishinaabe azhigwa ani-maajaad, mii dash imaa
mindimooyenyibaneg gaa-ayaajig owapii, mii iw gaa-
ikidowaad, "Gindidawiziwan ojichaagowaan aano-go gii-
chaagidenig inow owiiyawiwaan. Mii-go imaa ge-izhi-
atooyegiban dibishkoo-go imaa zhingishing awiya."

Mii-go dibishkoo gaye a'aw gaa-kiishkigaadezhond, mii imaa
dabazhish inow ozidan da-gii-ayaamagadinigoban, mii imaa
bashkwegino-makizinan achigaadenig. Gii-kiishkininjiizhond
awiya, mii-ko a'aw asemaa echigaazod imaa oninjiing, mii-go
ge-izhi-gashkapijigaazonid imaa da-achigaazonid inow
asemaan.

Mii iw izhinikaazowin Waasigwan imaa ani-aabajitooyaang
ani-dazhindamaang i'iw maajaa'iwewin. Gaawiin igo awiya
a'aw Waasigwan gaa-izhinikaazod indazhimaasiwaanaan
omaa. Booch i'iw izhinikaazowin da-ni-aabajichigaadeg omaa
endazhinjigaadeg i'iw maajaa'iwewin.

Booch a'aw mayaajaa'iwed da-ayaawaad ge-naadamaagojin
imaa maajaa'iwed aniindi-go da-baa-izhaad oda-wiijiiwigoon.
Ogikendaanaawaa wiinawaa ge-izhichigeng da-ozhiitaang.
Gaawiin dash memwech a'aw mayaajaa'iwed oda-
babaamendanziin gegoo, mii-go imaa weweni da-
giizisijigaadenig imaa ayaabajichigaadenig imaa maajaa'iweng.

Once I did a funeral for a couple that died in a house fire. There were very few remains left. The remains were placed in vases, with each vase being placed into their individual caskets. As we were getting ready to place the items in the caskets that usually go with the person, the old ladies that were present at the time said, "Their spirits are whole even though their bodies are burned. Place those items inside there as if their bodies were lying there."

This is the same for an amputee who has had his or her legs removed. The moccasins can be placed where the feet would have been. If someone had their fingers removed since this is where the tobacco is usually placed, the tobacco can be wrapped up in cloth, creating a small bundle and placed in the casket.

I want to talk about the name Waasigwan that we are using as we talk about a funeral. There is no one named Waasigwan that we are actually referring to here. It is only put there because we need a name to use as we discuss what goes into these funerals.

The one who is doing the funeral will also have to have his helpers wherever he goes; they need to go with him. They know what needs to be done to prepare for each funeral. That way the one who is doing the funeral does not have to worry about whether or not everything has been placed in order that he will use during the course of the funeral.

Booch a'aw waa-maajaa'iwed zakab da-izhi-ayaad imaa
odinendamowining naa biinjina. Gaawiin igo wenipanasinoon
maajaa'iwed awiya. Ishke ingiw mindimooyenyibaneg gaa-
inaawaad inow gaa-naadamawinijin, "Weweni ganawenimik
a'aw waa-ni-gaagiigidod. Weweni gaye i'iw ge-minikwed gidaa-
atamawaawaa. Weweni giizhaa gidaa-ozisidamawaawaa ge-
aabajitood a'aw ge-maajaa'iwed da-biindigadooyeg imaa waa-
tanakamagak miinawaa da-azhe-atooyeg azhigwa imaa ani-
giizhiitaang. Mii dash gaawiin gegoo oda-wanishkwe'igosiin
a'aw waa-maajaa'iwed. Weweni-go omaa odinendamowining
da-ni-izhi-ayaad. Mii iw ge-naadamaagod imaa azhigwa imaa
ani-bazigwiid da-ni-maajitaad da-ni-maajaa'iwed."

Ishke inow oshkaabewisan odayaawaan, mii inow ge-
naadamaagojin inow asemaan giizhaa da-ozhishimaawaad
miinawaa da-maada'ookiiwaad. Miinawaa oda-baa-
wiijiiwigoon inow ikwewan da-naadamaagewaad i'iw
wiisiniwin da-dazhiikamowaad. Miinawaa giishpin ikwewid
a'aw waa-ni-maajaa'ind, mii eta-go inow ikwewan ge-
ozhiitaa'igojin. Gaawiin a'aw inini gegoo imaa odaa-
dazhiikanziin i'iwapii.

Mii iw akeyaa gaa-izhi-gikinoo'amaagoowiziyaan. Aanind a'aw
Anishinaabe bakaan gii-izhi-gikinoo'amawaa. Gaawiin gaye da-
aanawendamawag i'iw akeyaa gaa-izhi-gikinoo'amawind
bakaan awiya. Mii eta-go wenji-ozhibii'amaan ow akeyaa gaa-
izhi-gikinoo'amaagoowiziyaan i'iw-sa da-ayaang a'aw
Anishinaabe ge-ni-aabajitoopan ayaanzig ge-ondiniged da-ni-
gikendang i'iw maajaa'iwewin ezhiwiinjigaadeg.

Wii-wawiingeziyeg miinawaa debinaak wii-ni-izhichigesiweg,
mii iw ge-izhichigeyegiban. Weweni asemaa gidaa-bi-
ininimawimin niin miinawaa Ombishkebines dabwaa-
aabajitooyeg omaa gaa-ozhibii'amaang. Ishke dash mii imaa
weweni bimiwidooyeg gaa-izhi-gikinoo'amaagoowiziyang

The one who is doing the funeral has to be at peace within and within his mind. It is not easy for someone to talk at a funeral. Those old ladies told the ones who help me, "Take good care of the one that will be talking at the funeral. Make sure you place something by him to drink. Set everything up ahead of time that he will use. Bring those items into the funeral site and also put them all away when the funeral is over. That way nothing will disturb the one that will be doing the talking and he will be able to think clearly as he gets up to talk."

He also has helpers that will assist him. They will lay out the tobacco ahead of time and also pass the tobacco out. There should also be ladies that will go along and help by taking care of the food. If the deceased is a female, it is only the female helpers that will get her prepared. A man should not touch anything around the casket at that time.

This is the way that I have been taught. Other Anishinaabe have been taught another way. I am not discounting what others have been taught. The only reason I am writing what I have been taught is to make this information available for the Anishinaabe to learn when they do not have source for learning how to do a traditional funeral

If you want to be thorough and not handle this half-heartedly, this is what you can do. You can hand tobacco to Chato and myself before putting this information to actual use. Doing this, you are also continuing to carry on our teaching as Anishinaabe by also extending your tobacco for this

anishinaabewiyang da-izhichigeyang, mii imaa ge-ondinigeyeg
da-ni-naadamaagoowiziyeg ingiw Manidoog
gidanaadamaagowaag da-ni-wawiingeziyeg azhigwa ani-
maajitaayeg ani-maajaa'iweyeg.

information. This is the where you will get your help; the
Manidoog will help you to be efficient as you start to do these
funerals.

2 BABAA-MAWADISANG I'IW AKI

2.1 Wiindamawindwaa eyaajig imaa da-naabishkaagewaad inow asemaan.

Mii imaa asemaa naa wiisiniwin achigaadeg azhigwa awiya gaa-ishkwaa-ayaad, mii iw ani-bangishimod a'aw giizis apii zagaswe'iding. Mii-go endaso-onaagoshig biinish iwidi abiitawind awiya ani-zagaswe'iding.

Mii a'aw asemaa gii-maada'ookiing miinawaa i'iw wiisiniwin gii-kiizisijigaadeg imaa michisagong.

Mii iw gii-paa-maada'ookiing a'aw asemaa naa gaye gii-kiizisijigaadeg i'iw wiisiniwin. Mii dash a'aw asemaa miinawaa i'iw wiisiniwin wenji-achigaadeg, mii imaa weweni ani-doodaagod inow odinawemaaganan a'aw Waasigwan besho gii-ni-inendaagwak da-ni-aanjikiid.

Ishke dash azhigwa weweni gaa-naabishkaageng a'aw asemaa, mii imaa da-ni-gaandoweyaan da-ni-dazhimag enagimind a'aw asemaa biinish gaye i'iw wiisiniwin da-ni-dazhindamaan.

Weweni naabishkaagedaa a'aw asemaa.

Mii-go maa minik akawe inwewetooyaan.

2 PRE-FUNERAL FEASTS

2.1 Tell those present to smoke the tobacco.

This is the feast that is held at dusk immediately after someone has passed, during those evenings leading up to the Wake.

Tobacco has been passed out and the food has been set out on the floor.

The tobacco has been passed out and the food has been laid out. The reason the tobacco and food is being placed here is because Waasigwan's close relatives are doing him good as it gets close to that time for him to change worlds.

As soon as the tobacco has been accepted I will go on to talk about what the tobacco is designated for and I also will go on to talk about the food.

Let's accept that tobacco in a good way.

That is all I will say for now.

2.2 Dazhinjigaazod enagimind a'aw asemaa biinish gaye wiisiniwin dazhinjigaadeg.

Mii imaa ani-wiindamaageng ezhi-gaagiigidong ani-dazhimind a'aw asemaa naa i'iw wiisiniwin echigaadeg. Mii imaa ani-wiidoopamind a'aw gaa-ishkwaa-ayaad megwaa maa babaamaadizid baa-mawadisaadang i'iw aki.

Ishke dash mii iw gii-maadaabasod a'aw asemaa, mii-go iwidi enabiwaad gakina ingiw Manidoog eni-inaabasod a'aw asemaa.

Mii imaa ge-ondiniged a'aw Waasigwan da-ni-naadamaagoowizid megwaa maa babaamaadizid baa-mawadisaadang o'ow aki, naa gaye azhigwa iwidi epiitawigendang da-ni-naazikaaged wenda-onaajiwang gaa-miinigoowizid a'aw Anishinaabe ge-ni-izhaad gegoo izhiwebizid.

Ishke dash minochigewag ingiw zayaagi-inawendaasojig gaabige ani-niigaaninaawaad inow odasemaawaan ininamawaawaad inow Manidoon. Mii-go ani-apiichitaayaang da-ni-asigishing dibishkoo enabiwaad ingiw Manidoog.

Minochigewag debinaak izhichigesigwaa ingiw zayaagi-inawendaasojig. Ishke gaawiin debinaak ingiw Manidoog gii-izhichigesiiwag inigokwekamig gaa-atoowaad ge-ni-naadamaagod a'aw Anishinaabe i'iwapii inendaagozid da-ni-aanjikiid.

Ishke nebowa gii-achigaade ge-naadamaagod a'aw Waasigwan ani-apiichitaad miinawaa geget onaajiwanini iwidi waa-ni-izhaad.

32

2.2. Tell what the tobacco is designated for and talk for the food.

This section explains how you talk for the tobacco and food that is being offered up. It is at this time that the food is being shared with the spirit of the deceased as he travels about.

The tobacco has gone out to all the Manidoog where they sit.

It is from there that Waasigwan will get his help as he travels about revisiting the Earth, and also when he decides to make his journey to that beautiful place that the Anishinaabe have been given to go to when something happens to them.

The close relatives are doing good by handing their tobacco to the Manidoog immediately. As we go along the tobacco will collect where those Manidoog sit.

It is good that the close relatives are doing this in an efficient manner. The Manidoog did a thorough job by putting so much in place to help the Anishinaabe when it is time for them to change worlds.

A lot has been put in place to help Waasigwan as he goes and it is also a beautiful place where he is going.

Ishke dash gaye ani-inaabasod a'aw asemaa enabiwaad ingiw Manidoog, gimiigwechiwi'aanaanig gii-miinigoowiziyang da-ni-wiidoopamang gidinawemaaganinaan azhigwa gegoo gaa-ni-izhiwebizid. Ishke naadamaagoowiziwag besho enawendaasojig okwi'idiwaad owapii endaso-dibik zagaswe'iding. Ishke zanagad wasadawendang awiya, gaawiin izhi-gozigwanisini i'iw owasidawendamowiniwaa bi-naazikaagowaad zhewenimigowaajin. Ishke gaye mii owapii bi-naazikaagowaad inow Anishinaaben eyaanijin omaa endanakiiwaad biindigadoonid i'iw wiisiniwin naadamaagowaad. Ishke dash naadamaagoowiziwag ingiw wesadawendangig waabamaawaad inow Anishinaaben zhawenimigowaad bi-naazikaagowaad. Mii gaye i'iw ge-ni-mikwendamowaad oniigaaniimiwaang agana-go da-izhi-gozigwaninig owasidawendamowiniwaa. Mii iw gaa-onji-gikinoo'amaagoowiziyang da-naadamawang a'aw giwiiji-anishinaabeminaan i'iwapii ani-gagwaadagitood.

Ishke dash enagimind a'aw asemaa gaye ginanaandomaanaanig ingiw Manidoog weweni da-ganawenimaawaad iniw zayaagi-inawendaasonijin iniw wesidaawendaminijin weweni da-ganawenimaawaad epiitakamigiziyang.

Ishke zanagad, gaawiin wenipanasinoon. Miinawaa daa-wii-naadamaagoowiziwag weweni da-ni-odaapinamowaad gaa-inaakonigewaad ingiw Manidoog o'owapii besho gii-inendaagozid a'aw Waasigwan da-ni-aanjikiid.

Ishke dash gaa-izhi-gikinoo'amaagoowiziyang anishinaabewiyang niiyo-dibik awiya ganawenjigaazo azhigwa gegoo gii-izhiwebizid. Mii dash o'owapii babaamaadizid babaa-mawadisaadang aaniindi-go gii-paa-ayaad megwaa maa gii-pibizhaagiid omaa akiing.

As the tobacco goes to where those Manidoog sit, we are thanking them for giving us the ability to eat with our relative once they have passed on. It is helpful for those that are grieving to get together with others and feast each night. It is difficult when someone is mourning, but it lightens the burden of their grief when others come to show their support at the time of these feasts. This is also the time that community members bring in their food to help out and show their compassion for the family who lost a loved one. It helps the family who has lost their loved one when they see the Anishinaabe come to show their compassion. That is what they will remember in the future and it will lighten the load of their grief. That is why we were taught to offer our support to our fellow Anishinaabe when they are going through a difficult time.

The tobacco is being put, asking that the Manidoog watch over the close relatives and those that are grieving as we go though the course of this funeral.

It is difficult, it is not easy. May the close relatives be helped to accept the decision made by the Manidoog that Waasigwan is to change worlds soon.

This is the teaching that we were given as Anishinaabe—that the body is held over for four nights. During that time the spirit of the individual travels about revisiting every place that they have been while on this Earth.

Ishke dash mii iw Waasigwan eni-izhichigegwen. Ishke dash akawe weweni niwii-wiindamawaa a'aw Waasigwan, "Azhigwa babaamaadiziyan baa-mawadisaadaman ow aki, gego babaamenimaaken ingiw besho enawemajig. Gidaa-inigaa'aag."

Ishke dash i'iw wiisiniwin omaa gaa-achigaadeg, gaawiin ingoji apagizonjigaadesinoon. Mii owapii weweni da-ni-wiidoopamang epiitawigendang waa-naganinang.

Ishke dash ingiw akiwenziiyibaneg omaa gii-ni-gaagiigidowaad, mii imaa gii-ni-ayaangwaamimaawaad iniw zayaagi-inawendaasonijin "Ayaangwaamizig da-ni-odaapinameg i'iw wiisiniwin. Ishke oda-minwendaan waabandang weweni ani-odaapinameg i'iw wiisiniwin, mii-go gaye wiin ge-ni-izhichiged. Odaapinanzig awiya, mii-go gaye wiin gaawiin oda-odaapinanziin. Biinish gaye gego agwajiing odaa-izhiwidoosiin i'iw wiisiniwin awiya, miinawaa gaye gidaa-wii-manaajitoonaawaa, gego omaa michisagong daa-wii-pangisinzinoon."

Ishke dash gaye ani-maadaabasod a'aw asemaa, mii iwidi ge-ni-inaabasod a'aw Manidoo epenimod a'aw Anishinaabe ani-asemaaked. Mii dash a'aw Giganaan ezhi-wiinind. Mii a'aw ge-ni-nanaa'isidood imaa giishpin gegoo ani-waniikeyaang ani-waniwebinigeyaang. Weweni dash igo da-aawang i'iw akeyaa ezhi-bagosendamang omaa okwi'idiyang.

Mii-go ge-izhi-odaapinamegiban i'iw wiisiniwin.

That is what Waasigwan is doing. It is here that I am going to tell Waasigwan, "As you travel and revisit this Earth, do not bother your close relatives. You could hurt them."

The food that has been put here is not sent anywhere. It is at this time we will share in a meal with the one that is going to leave us at his own leisure.

When the old men talked here they encouraged the close relatives, "Please make every effort to accept the food. Waasigwan will like seeing you accepting the food and he too will accept the food. If you do not accept the food he also will not accept the food. Also nobody should take the food outside and you should handle the food with care so it does not fall on the floor."

The tobacco is also going out to that Manidoo the Anishinaabe rely on when they offer up their tobacco. That is the Manidoo that is named Giganaan. She is the one that will correct anything if we were to forget something or make an error. That way everything will be accomplished that we wish to do through this ceremony as we are gathered here.

You can all accept the food now.

3 ABIITAWIND

3.1 Wiindamawindwaa eyaajig imaa da-naabishkaagewaad inow asemaan.

Mii imaa da-ni-wiindamaageng da-ni-naabishkaageng a'aw asemaa gaa-maada'ookiing. Mii dash gaye da-ni-wiindamaageng waa-ni-izhichigeng azhigwa ani-giizhiitaad gakina awiya imaa ani-naabishkaaged inow asemaan.

- *Mii imaa gii-kiizisijigaadeg i'iw obimiwanaan a'aw waa-ni-maajaad. Mii imaa niiwing da-aanzikang iniw biizikiganan gii-achigaadeg. Mii imaa giziingwe'on, giziingwe'oons, biinish gaye inow asemaan. Mii imaa da-gashkapijigaadeg imaa maamandoogwaasoning. Mii imaa achigaadeg anaamayi'ii i'iw jiibayi-makak michisagong iwidi ezhizideshing waa-ni-maajaad.*

- *Mii iw bimiwanaan ge-miinind a'aw genawendamaaged inow Bwaani-dewe'iganan. Mii dash ezhinaagozid a'aw Bwaani-dewe'igan. Mii imaa ogijayi'ii miskobii'igaazod naa ozhaawashkonaanzod. Mii dash imaa naawayi'ii ozaawaabii'igaazod. Mii dash iw giishpin ayaasigwaa ingiw Manidoo-dewe'iganag maagizhaa gaye ezhichigesigwaa endanakiijig imaa, mii-go ge-izhi-miinind awiya waasa wenjiid miinawaa ge-minokang iniw biizikiganan. Mii gaye ge-izhi-miinind gakina inow biizikiganan gaa-ayaang gaa-ni-maajaad.*

- *Mii gaye imaa ogijayi'ii i'iw jiibayi-makak ozhibii'igaazonid inow odoodeman gii-ozhibii'igaazonid imaa nabagisagong.*

3 WAKE

3.1 Tell those present to smoke the tobacco.

It is here that everyone is told to accept the tobacco that has been passed out on behalf of the Manidoog. It is then that everyone is told what will happen once everyone has either smoked the tobacco or put it in the fire.

- *The bundle has been made for the one who is about to depart. In that bundle, there are four changes of clothing, along with a towel, a washcloth, and a pouch of tobacco. A quilt will be used to bundle up everything and it will be placed on the floor at the foot of the casket.*

- *The bundle will be given to a drum keeper, one who takes care of a Sioux drum, with the red and blue paint with a yellow strip down the middle. In other communities it may be the custom just to send it to someone from a distance that will use the clothing. The remainder of the clothing will also get sent with whoever takes the bundle.*

- *His or her clan marker is placed on top of the casket. The clan of the deceased is etched out on a board.*

Aanjikiing: An Anishinaabe Traditional Funeral

Mii iw gii-paa-maada'oonigooyeg a'aw asemaa.

Mii imaa da-ni-naabishkaageyeg weweni.

Mii a'aw asemaa ininamawindwaa ingiw Manidoog, ge-
onjikaamagadinig a'aw Waasigwan da-ni-naadamaagoowizid
megwaa maa babaamaadizid baa-mawadisaadang i'iw aki naa
gaye epiitawigendang azhigwa iwidi da-ni-naazikaaged
"Gaagige-minawaanigoziwining" ezhi-wiinjigaadeg.

Ishke dash omaa ani-giizhi-naabishkaageyang, mii dash imaa
da-ni-gaandoweyaan, mii dash imaa da-ni-wiikwajitooyaan da-
ni-wiindamaageyaan enagimind a'aw asemaa.

Biinish gaye da-ni-waawiindamawag a'aw Waasigwan
miinawaa gaye giinawaa indinawemaaganidog gaa-
onjikaamagak-sa o'ow gii-miinigoowizid a'aw Anishinaabe
o'ow akeyaa da-ni-izhichiged, naa biinish gaye gii-
miinigoowizid ge-ni-izhaad gegoo izhiwebizid.

Ani-giizhiitaayaan, mii dash imaa gaye da-ni-dazhindamaan
i'iw wiisiniwin.

Mii-go maa akawe minik inwewetooyaan.

Weweni naabishkaagedaa.

The tobacco has just been passed out to you all.

It is now that you all will take the tobacco on behalf of the Manidoog in a good way.

It is that tobacco that is being handed to the Manidoog, the source from which Waasigwan will be helped while he is traveling out and about visiting the earth and also when he chooses to approach over to that place called "Land of Everlasting Happiness."

When we are finished taking the tobacco in for the Manidoog, it is then I will go on to talk further, and I will try to tell what the tobacco is intended for.

I will also go on to tell Waasigwan and also you my relatives where this all came from, when the Anishinaabe was given this particular ceremony and was given a place to go when anything happens to him.

When I am finished, I will also go on to talk about the food.

This is all that I will say for now.

Let's all take the tobacco in a good way for the Manidoog.

3.2 Dazhinjigaazod enagimind a'aw asemaa biinish gaye wiisiniwin dazhinjigaadeg. Naa gaye wiindamaageng gaa-onjikaamagak gii-miinigoowizid a'aw Anishinaabe o'ow akeyaa da-ni-izhichiged.

Mii-go miinawaa da-ni-dazhimind a'aw asemaa, mii-go gakina awiya gaa-naabishkaaged inow asemaan.

Mii dash gii-maadaabasod a'aw asemaa.

Gaawiin ingoji da-aanzweyaabasosiin enabiwaad ingiw Manidoog.

Mii imaa ge-ondiniged-sa a'aw Waasigwan da-ni-naadamaagoowizid azhigwa epiitawigendang da-ni-naazikaaged iwidi wenda-onaajiwang, "Gaagige-minawaanigoziwining," ezhi-wiinjigaadeg. Mii omaa weweni da-ni-naadamaagoowizid-sa gii-inenimigod inow Manidoon o'owapii da-ni-aanjikiid.

Ishke dash mii o'ow enagimind a'aw asemaa. Weweni omaa gidoodawaanaanig ingiw Manidoog, inigokwekamig omaa gaa-atoowaad ge-ni-naadamaagod a'aw Anishinaabe o'owapii inendaagozid da-ni-aanjikiid.

Ishke weweni oda-ni-naadamaagon a'aw Waasigwan iwidi ge-ni-apiichitaad da-ni-naazikaaged eni-izhaad a'aw gidanishinaabeminaan gaagwiinawaabaminaagozid omaa akiing.

3.2 Tell what the tobacco is designated for and talk for the food. Also, tell the origin of this ceremony.

This is the second time you need to get up to talk and everyone has completed their smoking and others have placed their tobacco in the fire.

The tobacco has now gone out.

There is no place that the tobacco will not go; it will reach all the Manidoog where they sit.

It is from there that Waasigwan will get his help once he decides to approach that beautiful place over there called, "Land of Everlasting Happiness." It is here that he will be helped, since the Manidoog decided it was his time to change worlds.

This is what the tobacco is designated for. We are doing those Manidoog good; there is a lot that they put here to help the Anishinaabe when it is meant for him to change worlds.

That is what will help Waasigwan in a good way as he goes along and approaches over there where our Anishinaabe go when they are no longer seen here on Earth.

Ishke dash giizhaa omaa weweni gidoodawaanaanig ingiw
Manidoog-sa weweni-go da-ni-gaakiizhiitaayang waa-ni-
izhichigeyang, da-ni-bitaakoshkanziwang gegoo, weweni-go
da-ni-naadamaagoowizid a'aw Waasigwan da-ni-
gaakiizhiikang-sa da-ni-aanjikiid.

Mii gaye enagimind a'aw asemaa, odaa-wii-shawenimigowaan
inow Manidoon ingiw besho enawendaasojig, weweni odaa-
wii-kanawenimigowaan omaa epiitakamigiziyang noongom
naa-go biinish gaye waabanokeyang.

Ishke zanagad geget, gaawiin wenipanasinoon.

Odaa-wii-shawenimigowaan dash inow Manidoon gaye
oniigaaniimiwaang mino-ayaawin da-ni-miinigoowiziwaad
naa-go gaye biinish weweni da-ni-naadamaagoowiziwaad-sa
weweni da-ni-odaapinamowaad gaa-inaakonigewaad ingiw
Manidoog-sa o'owapii gii-inenimind a'aw Waasigwan da-ni-
aanjikiid.

Biinish gaye a'aw asemaa ani-dazhimag, gaawiin niwii-
wanenimaasiin a'aw Manidoo epenimod a'aw Anishinaabe ani-
asemaaked, wenjida o'ow akeyaa noongom ani-izhichigeyang.

Ishke mii iw iwidi ge-ni-inaabasod a'aw asemaa a'aw Giganaan
ezhi-wiinind gaye a'aw Dibiki-giizis.

Mii a'aw Manidoo gaa-pi-wiindamaaged wii-naadamawaad
inow Anishinaaben aaniin igo ani-izhichiged ani-asemaaked.

Ishke giishpin omaa gegoo waniikeyaang, waniwebinigeyaang,
mii a'aw Manidoo ge-ni-nanaa'isidood.

We are doing the Manidoog good ahead of time so that we finish in a good way what we are doing, and that we don't bump into something as we go along, and also so that Waasigwan is properly helped on his way toward finishing his changing of worlds.

The tobacco is also being put to so that those Manidoo show compassion towards the close relatives. It is our wish that the Manidoog take care of the close relatives as we go along doing this and also tomorrow.

It is certainly difficult, it is not easy.

May those Manidoog have compassion for them, and that in their future they be given good health, and that they also be helped to accept in a good way the decision the Manidoog made that it was at this time Waasigwan was meant to change worlds.

Also as I am talking about the tobacco, I don't want to forget the Manidoo that Anishinaabe rely on when they offer their tobacco to the Manidoog, especially in what we are doing now.

The tobacco will go to the Manidoo known as Giganaan who is the Moon.

She is the Manidoo that came and told that she will help the Anishinaabe in whatever way they offer their tobacco.

If we were to forget or omit something in what we are doing as we go along, that is the Manidoo that will correct it.

Mii dash imaa ge-ondiniged a'aw Waasigwan da-ni-wawiinge'oonwewizid-sa inigokwekamig imaa gaa-achigaadeg-sa ge-naadamaagod a'aw Anishinaabe o'owapii inendaagozid da-ni-aanjikiid.

Biinish gaye a'aw asemaa eni-inaabasod gakina enabiwaad ingiw Manidoog, nigaagiizomaag giishpin omaa inenimigooyaan da-ni-aanikanootamaageyaan omaa eni-dazhinjigaadeg. Gaawiin nibaapinendanziin i'iw gaa-ina'oonwewiziyang anishinaabewiyang.

Nebowa a'aw Anishinaabe ogii-waniba'igon i'iw akeyaa gaa-miinigod inow Manidoon da-ni-inwed.

Geget gigii-aanooji'igoomin wii-wayezhimigooyang anishinaabewiyang.

Ishke dash mii eta wenji-izhichigeyaan omaa inendamaan da-ondiniged a'aw Anishinaabe da-ni-naadamaagoowizid.

Biinish gaye niin iwidi ishkodeng ingii-asaa indasemaam.

Mii a'aw gaye niin epagizondamawagig ingiw Manidoog-sa omaa weweni da-ni-naadamaagoowiziyaan da-ni-wawiingeziyaan da-ni-ganoodamawag a'aw Waasigwan.

Ishke mii o'o maamaw-zanagak iko ani-gaagiigidod awiya. Gaawiin wenipanasinoon.

Mii dash owapii wii-ni-maajitaayaan ani-waawiindamoonaan Waasigwan, naa-go gaye giinawaa indinawemaaganidog o'ow-sa gaa-onjikaamagak gii-miinigoowizid Anishinaabe o'ow akeyaa da-ni-izhichiged, biinish gaye gii-miinigoowizid ge-ni-izhaad gegoo izhiwebizid.

It is from there that Waasigwan will get everything that was so abundantly put in place to help the Anishinaabe when it is meant for him to change worlds.

As the tobacco goes to where all the Manidoog sit, I ask for compassion if it is meant for me to translate what is being said here. I am not being disrespectful to what we have been given as Anishinaabe.

The language we have been given to speak by the Manidoog has eluded many of our Anishinaabe.

There was a movement to deceive us as Anishinaabe.

The only reason I translate here is with the idea of helping our fellow Anishinaabe.

I also put my tobacco in the fire.

I also send my tobacco to the Manidoog to help me be efficient as I talk for Waasigwan.

This is the most difficult talk for anyone to do. It is not easy.

It is now that I will begin to tell you, Waasigwan, and also you, my relatives, where this ceremony came from, and also when the Anishinaabe were given a place to go when something happens to them.

Ishke ingiw akiwenziiyibaneg ogii-tibaadodaanaawaa; geget a'aw Anishinaabe ishkweyaang gaa-ayaad mewinzha gii-kidimaagizi.

Ishke gegoo gii-izhiwebizid, gaawiin ogii-ayaanziin ge-ni-izhaad. Gii-kaagiiwozhitoo. Mii-go iwidi enaanimadinig gaa-izhaanid inow ojichaagwan.

Ishke dash gii-niizhiwag ingiw Manidoog gaa-naadamaagejig.

Ishke a'aw Manidoo enawemang giningwanisinaan Wenabozho, mii a'aw bezhig gaa-naadamaaged, miinawaa gaye inow odoozhiman.

Ishke dash ogii-wiij'ayaawaan inow odoozhiman.

Ishke dash aabiding babaamaadizid a'aw Wenabozho baa-giiwosed gaa-izhi-moonenimaad gegoo gii-izhiwebizinid inow odoozhiman.

Wayeshkad gii-noondawag a'aw akiwenzii gii-tibaajimod "Ganabaj ogii-nisigoon awiya," gii-ikido

Mii iw imaa gii-pi-giiwed a'aw Wenabozho, geget dash gaawiin gii-ayaasiiwan inow odoozhiman.

Mii imaa gii-nanaamadabid a'aw Wenabozho.

Gaa-niiyo-giizhigadinig gaa-izhi-noondawaad bi-naazikaagod.

Mii-go gaa-izhi-goshkwaakoshkang i'iw aki. Aaniish naa Manidoo a'aw. Aana-wii-pi-biindigewan dash imaa gii-taawaad.

Mii dash gaa-izhi-inaad, "Gego omaa bi-biindigeken. Gegoo da-izhiwebad omaa eyaayaang."

48

Those old men talked about how pitiful the Anishinaabe were long time ago.

When anything happened to them, the Anishinaabe did not have anywhere to go. They wandered with no direction. Wherever the wind blew that is where their spirit went.

There were two Manidoog that helped.

One of those that helped us was that Manidoo we are related too, our nephew Wenabozho, and also his nephew.

He lives with his nephew.

One time when Wenabozho was out traveling and hunting he sensed something had happened to his nephew.

The first time I heard this old man talk about it, he said he thinks someone had killed him.

It was then that Wenabozho came home and, sure enough, his nephew was not there.

There Wenabozho sat.

On the fourth day he heard his spirit approaching.

He shook the world. He was a Manidoo after all. He wanted to come in where they lived.

And then he told him, "Don't come in our home. Something will happen here."

Mii dash owapii a'aw Wenabozho gii-mikwenimaad ezhi-inigaazinid inow odanishinaabeman, gaa-izhi-gagwejimaad inow odoozhiman, "Gidaa-ni-ozhitoon ina i'iw miikanens ge-ni-izhaad a'aw gidanishinaabeminaan gegoo ani-izhiwebizid?"

Mii dash geget gii-nakomigod.

Mii dash iwidi ningaabii'anong akeyaa gaa-ni-izhaad gii-ni-ozhitood i'iw miikanens.

Ginwenzh gii-ni-dazhitaa.

Azhigwa dash iwidi maa minik gaa-ni-dagoshimoonod mii iw iwidi gii-ni-gagwejimaad inow Wenabozhoyan "Mii na minik?"

"Gaawiin" ogii-igoon "Awas igo izhaan".

Mii-go miinawaa gii-ni-maajaad.

Mii-go dibishkoo miinawaa ginwenzh gii-ni-dazhitaa.

Azhigwa dash ani-noogitaad iwidi eko-niizhing ani-gagwedwed miinawaa "Mii na minik?"

Mii-go gaawiin ogii-tebisewendanziin a'aw Wenabozho.

Mii-go miinawaa gii-ni-maajaad.

Ginwenzh gii-ni-dazhitaa gii-ni-ozhitood i'iw miikanens miinawaa.

Azhigwa dash ani-noogitaad iwidi eko-nising ani-gagwedwed miinawaa "Mii na minik?" Mii i'iw gaawiin mashi ogii-tebisewendanziin a'aw Wenabozho.

This is when Wenabozho remembered how pitiful his Anishinaabe were and asked his nephew, "Can you make that path and that place our Anishinaabe can go to when something happens to them?"

He agreed to do so.

He went toward the west and made that path.

He worked on it for a long time.

After he had been working on that path for some time he stopped and asked Wenabozho "Is this far enough?"

"No, go farther." he told him.

And then he took off again.

He worked on that path for a long time again.

After he stopped over there for a second time he asked, "Is this enough?"

Wenabozho was still not content.

So he went on again.

He went on to work a long time on that path again.

After he stopped over there for the third time he asked, "Is this enough?" And still Wenabozho was not content.

Mii dash igo miinawaa gii-ni-maajaad.

Azhigwa ginwenzh gaa-ni-dazhitaad iwidi gii-ni-dazhiikang i'iw miikanens, azhigwa dash ani-noogitaad iwidi eko-niiwing ani-gagwedwed miinawaa, "Mii na minik?" Mii dash owapii bijiinag gii-tebisewendang a'aw Wenabozho.

Ishke dash mii iw wenji-ayaang a'aw Anishinaabe ge-ni-izhaad gegoo izhiwebizid onji inow Manidoon gii-shawenimigod.

Ishke dash Waasigwan, waabanokeyang, mii imaa da-ni-waawiindamaagooyan isa gaa-inaabamind a'aw Manidoo owapii gii-ni-ozhitood i'iw miikanens.

Mii dash owapii wii-ni-dazhindamaan i'iw wiisiniwin.

Ishke i'iw wiisiniwin gaawiin ingoji apagizonjigaadesinoon owapii.

Akawe igo omaa weweni gida-wiidoopamaanaan, epiitawigendang waa-naganinang.

Ishke gaa-izhi-gikinoo'amaagoowiziyang anishinaabewiyang, mii ow niiyo-dibik ganawenjigaazod awiya.

Mii owapii babaamaadizid baa-mawidisaadang i'iw aki aaniindi-go gii-pabaa-ayaad megwaa maa gii-pibizhaagiid omaa akiing.

Ishke dash ingiw akiwenziiyibaneg gii-ni-gaagiigidowaad, mii omaa gii-ni-ayaangwaamimaawaad iniw zayaagi-inawendaasonijin da-ni-ayaangwaamiziwaad da-ni-odaapinamowaad i'iw wiisiniwin. Ishke oda-minwendaan Waasigwan waabandang weweni odaapinigaadeg i'iw

So he went on again.

Now he had been working on that path for quite some time, after he stopped over there for the fourth time he asked, "Is this enough?" Finally Wenabozho was content.

That is why the Anishinaabe have a place to go when something happens to them, because of these Manidoog taking pity on the Anishinaabe.

Tomorrow you will be told, Waasigwan, what was seen as that Manidoo made that path.

It is at this time I will talk about the food.

The food is not being sent anywhere at this time.

It is at this time we will be having a meal with his spirit before he leaves us.

This is what we were taught as Anishinaabe, for four nights the individual is held over.

It is at that time he revisits every place he had been while he lived on this earth.

When those old men went on to talk, it was here that they stressed to the close relatives that they should make a special effort to accept the food. Waasigwan will like seeing everybody accepting the food, and he will do the same. If someone does not accept the food, he also will not accept the food.

wiisiniwin, mii-go ge-wiin ge-ni-izhichiged. Ishke odaapinanzig awiya, mii-go gaye wiin gaawiin oda-odaapinanziin.

Ayaangwaamizig aano-go ezhi-zanagak.

Biinish gaye gego awiya agwajiing odaa-wii-izhiwidoosiin i'iw wiisiniwin miinawaa manaajitoog gego imaa michisagong daa-wii-pangisinzinoon.

Ishke dash gaye gidaa-wii-mikwendaanaawaa baanimaa gakina awiya omaa gii-ni-giizhiitaad ani-odaapinang i'iw wiisiniwin, mii dash omaa da-ni-gaandoweyaan da-ni-wiikwajitooyaan da-ni-ganoonagwaa ingiw zayaagi-inawendaasojig.

Mii-go maa minik akawe inwewetooyaan

Mii-go ge-izhi-odaapinamegiban i'iw wiisiniwin.

Try even though it is difficult.

Also, nobody should take the food outside, and handle the food carefully so it does not drop on the floor.

You should also remember it is not until everyone here has finished eating that I can go on to talk to the close relatives.

That's all I am saying for now.

Now you can all eat.

4 BESHO ENAWENDAASOJIG

Mii imaa ani-ganoonindwaa besho enawendaasojig. Mii imaa ani-wiindamawindwaa ge-naadamaagowaad gaa-wanitaasojig.

Mii-ko owapii ingiw akiwenziiyibaneg gii-kanoonaawaad iniw zayaagi-inawendaasonijin Mii dash i'iw waa-ni-wiikwajitooyaan wii-ni-izhichigeyaan.

Mii ow naaniigaan waa-tazhindamaan geget onaajiwanini iwidi Waasigwan eni-izhaad.

Ishke gaawiin gegoo wiiyagasenh iwidi ayaamagasinoon, biinish gaye gakina gaa-ina'oonwewizid a'aw Anishinaabe enakamigizid, mii i'iw enakamigiziwaad iwidi geget minawaanigwad. Da-minawaanigozi iwidi Waasigwan.

Biinish gaye iwidi azhigwa eni-dagoshimoonod mii iwidi da-ni-waawaabamaad gakina inow odinawemaaganan gaa-minjinawezid gaye wiin. Mii-go ge-izhi-biijibatoowaad naa gaye ge-izhi-noodaagoziwaad ezhi-minwendamowaad waabamaawaad iwidi bi-dagoshimoononid Waasigwanan.

Ishke dash booch-go maa minik gida-gaagwiinawenimaawaa.

Mii-ko ingiw akiwenziiyibaneg ogii-tazhindaanaawaa, booch i'iw da-ayaamagak i'iw wasidaawendamowin omaa maa minik.

Ishke dash ogii-tazhindaanaawaa ingiw akiwenziiyibaneg, Ishke mii iwidi bagwaj ge-ni-izhaapan awiya da-ni-nasanaamod, ogii-izhi-wiindaanaawaa. Gida-noondaagowaag ingiw Manidoog. Gida-zhawenimigowaag. Gida-naadamaagowaag.

4 CLOSE RELATIVES TALK

This is where you speak directly to the family. They will be given advice about how to deal with their grief.

This was the time the old men usually talked to the close relatives. That's what I am going to try to do.

The first thing I want to talk about is how nice the place is that Waasigwan is going to.

There is no dust over there and everything the Anishinaabe was given to do ceremony-wise is happening with them up there and it is a really happy place. Waasigwan will be happy over there.

Also when he arrives over there he will see all his relatives that he has grieved for since they left. They will come running and laughing with joy as they see Waasigwan arrive over there.

Of course you are going to miss him for a length of time.

Those old men talked about how the grieving will be there for a period of time.

Those old men recommended that those who are grieving should go out in the woods and release their emotions. The Manidoog will hear you. They will take pity on you. They help you.

Ishke dash gaye booch-sa wiin igo maa minik gomaapii gidaa-bagidenimaawaa.

Ishke aabiji-minjiminaad inow odinawemaaganan a'aw Anishinaabe iwidi ezhaanid, gaawiin da-minawaanigozisiiwan gaye wiin iwidi. Mii-ko gaa-izhi-wiindamawindwaa.

Naa gaye gii-ni-waawiindamawaawag gaye ge-ni-izhichigewaad ingiw zayaagi-inawendaasojig.

Mii-ko gaa-inindwaa, "Gigizheb wiikwajitoog da-onishkaayeg da-waabameg a'aw giizis da-bi-zaagewed da-bi-mookiid. Naa gaye weweni doodaadizog wenaajiwang gidaa-biizikaanaawaa. Naa gego aabiji-nawagikwebikegon. Zhoomiingwetaw a'aw Anishinaabe bi-naazikook."

Ishke moozhag nimbi-noondawaag ingiw Anishinaabeg dazhindamowaad i'iw azhigwa gaa-wani'aawaad besho enawemaawaajin "Mii i'iw booch da-ni-boonitooyaan i'iw maagizhaa gaye nagamoyaan maagizhaa gaye niimiyaan akawe i'iw bezhig i'iw gikinoonowin da-baabii'oyaan miinawaa da-ni-izhichigeyaan iw akeyaa."

Gaawiin i'iw akeyaa gigii-izhi-gikinoo'amaagoosiimin anishinaabewiyang.

Gigii-ayaangwaamimigoomin da-wiikwajitooyang da-minawaanigoziyang, mii-go gaye wiin iwidi da-minawaanigozid a'aw gidinawemaaganinaan iwidi gaa-inendaagozid da-ni-aanjikiid.

Naa gaye gii-ni-waawiindamawaawag miinawaa gaye gii-gagiikimaawag ge-ni-izhichigewaad.

But you will also have to let him go at some point.

If the Anishinaabe continuously hold on to their relative that has gone over there, they will not be happy over there. That is what was told to them.

And they were told what to do as close relatives.

They were told, "Get up early and watch the sunrise. Do yourself good and wear something nice. And don't always have your head down. Smile as the Anishinaabe approach you."

Often I hear Anishinaabe say that once they have lost a close relative "I have to quit singing and dancing and I should wait one year before I do those things again."

That is not the way we were taught as Anishinaabe.

They encouraged us to try to be happy, and also our relative over there will be happy.

They were also taught what to do in their future.

Ishke ingiw Manidoog gigii-miinigonaanig anishinaabewiyang ge-inanjigeyang, ishke ingiw anooj igo ingiw awesiinyag waawaashkeshiwag, waaboozoog, biinish gaye ingiw giigoonyag, naa-go gaye i'iw manoomin, naa biinish gaye bagwaj imaa mayaajiiging.

Ishke dash gegoo omaa biinjina ayaamagad meshkawaamagak azhigwa gaa-wani'ang a'aw besho enawemang.

Gidaa-banaajitoomin i'iw baa-maamiginamang i'iw gaa-izhi-miinigoowiziyang da-inanjigeyang.

Akawe gidaa-asemaakemin giishpin wii-mamooyang, wii-tazhiikamang, wii-miijiyang i'iw gaa-miinigoowiziyang.

Ishke niwii-tazhindaan i'iw manoomin miinawaa zaagakiimagak misawendameg i'iw da-wii-miijiyeg i'iw oshki-manoomin, maagizhaa gaye misawendameg da-baa-maamiginameg i'iw manoomin. Akawe gidaa-anoonaawaa awiya-sa da-naadid i'iw manoomin da-ni-giizhiikang da-ni-giizizang. Mii dash imaa da-zhakamoonigooyeg i'iw manoomin miinawaa asemaa da-achigaazod.

Mii dash i'iw da-ni-maamiijiyegiban oshki-manoomin naa-go gaye da-naadiyegiban.

Mii iw akeyaa ge-izhichigeyegiban giishpin i'iw akeyaa izhi-misawendameg.

Mii i'iw gakina ge-doodameg i'iw gaa-izhi-miinigoowiziyang anishinaabewiyang da-inanjigeyang.

See, the Manidoog gave us as Anishinaabe the foods that we are to eat, such as the different animals: the deer, rabbits, also the fish, also the wild rice and including that which grows in the wild.

See there is something powerful within us once we have lost a close relative.

We could ruin what we were given to eat if we were to just go out and pick or harvest it.

We must first put our tobacco if we want to take, handle, or eat those foods which we were given as a people.

I am going to talk about when the wild rice appears again and you wish to eat fresh rice, or harvest it. First you should go out and ask someone to pick it, finish it and then cook it for you. It is then that you have to be spoon-fed the rice and a tobacco offering is made.

From there on out you can eat fresh rice or harvest it.

That is what you should do if that is what you desire to do.

That is what you have to do to all the things we were given as Anishinaabe people to eat.

Ishke ingiw akiwenziiyibaneg ikidowag, mii iw wenji-maneziyang nebowa gaa-izhi-miinigoowiziyang da-inanjigeyang, gaawiin obimiwidoosiin a'aw Anishinaabe geyaabi gaa-izhi-gikinoo'amawind.

Naa gaye gii-wiindamawaawag gaye ingiw bebiiwizhiiwijig ingiw abinoojinyag, gaawiin odaa-dazhiikawaasiin awiya.

Akawe da-baabii'o bezhig i'iw gikinoonowin da-ni-bimisemagak.

Naa gaye gii-wiindamawaawag gaye da-ganawaabandamowaad i'iw akeyaa ezhi-bimiwidoowaad i'iw bimaadiziwaad, wenjida i'iw besho gii-inendaagwadinig gii-wani'aawaad inow besho enawemaawaajin.

Ishke mewinzha ingiw akiwenziiyibaneg gii-maadaanagidoonoog gii-tazhindamowaad i'iw minikwewin, mii-go gaye dibishkoo i'iw anooj ani-aabajitood noongom a'aw bemaadizid wenda-noomage-apaginigod neshwanaaji'igod.

Ishke ani-onzaamiikang i'iw minikwewin naa anooj i'iw ayaabajitood noongom awiya, mii-go imaa da-ni-baataashing. Mii-go ge-ni-inaadizid oniigaaniiming, gii-inaawag.

Naa gaye naniizaanichige a'aw Anishinaabe ani-zhazhiibitang, Mii-go gaye wiin gaabige iwidi da-ni-izhaapan ani-dazhiikang neshwanaaji'igoyang.

Mii ow akeyaa gaa-izhi-gikinoo'amawindwaa gaye.

Naa gaye a'aw bezhig a'aw mindimooyenyiban, gii-zoongi-mide-ikwewi, gii-wiindamaage-sa omaa da-ni-dazhinjigaadeg i'iw gaye, ishke nebowa a'aw bemaadizid eni-izhiwebizid

The old men say that is why we are lacking a lot of those foods we have been given as Anishinaabe, because the Anishinaabe have not been following these teachings that have been given to them.

They were also told not to handle infants during that period.

They must wait one year before doing that.

They were also told to watch how they live their life, especially when they recently lost someone close to them.

See, those old men started talking long ago about alcohol, and also the drugs that are destroying lives today and slamming our people to the ground.

The Anishinaabe were told if they were to get into heavy alcohol or drug use they will get stuck in that life and that's the way they would continue to live, that is what they were told.

The Anishinaabe are messing with danger by doing that when they do not follow what they are being told. They too can journey over there quickly if they were to indulge in those things that mess up our lives.

That's the way they were taught also.

Also, this one old lady who was fourth degree Mide wanted the following to be told, it is common that as soon as families lose a

azhigwa gaa-ni-wani'aad inow besho enawemaajin, mii imaa
eni-gagwaadagi'idiwaad awenen waa-mamood i'iw gaa-
nagadang a'aw enendaagozid iwidi da-ni-aanjikiid.

Ishke a'aw mindimooyenyiban, mii iw gaa-tazhindang
maagizhaa gaye inow meshkwadooniganan, maagizhaa gaye
odaabaanan, maagizhaa gaye waakaa'igan.

Ishke gii-ikido a'aw mindimooyenyiban, gaawiin wiin gegoo
apiitendaagwasinoon iniw. Nawaj apiitendaagwad i'iw da-ni-
zhawenindiyang wenjida besho enawendaasoyang o'owapii
wani'ang a'aw besho enawemang.

Gii-ikido azhigwa enendaagoziyang gaye giinawind iwidi da-ni-
naazikaageyang, mii i'iw bimiwanaan ge-bimoondamang. Mii
imaa ani-maajiidooyang i'iw gakina wenaajiwang i'iw
zhewenimang a'aw giwiiji-bimaadiziiminaan, mii o'ow
maamaw-apiitendaagwak; gaawiin i'iw gida-ni-
maajiidoosiimin. Mii i'iw mindimooyenyiban gaa-tazhindang.

Ishke mii dash omaa eni-giizhiikamaan o'ow gaagiigidowin
eyaamagak.

Geget gimino-doodawaawaa a'aw Waasigwan.

Mii-go iwidi ge-ni-izhaad a'aw gidanishinaabeminaan eni-
izhaad gaagwiinawaabaminaagozid omaa akiing.

Ishke aanind a'aw Anishinaabe ani-aanawendang i'iw akeyaa
gaa-izhi-miinigoowiziyang, maazhichige geget.

Ishke bakaan izhi-maajaa'ind, gaawiin ingoji da-izhaasiin a'aw
Anishinaabe.

a close relative there is a lot of fighting over who gets to take the material things left behind by the deceased.

The old lady was talking about money, or maybe a car, or maybe a house.

That old lady said those material things were of no value. What is worth more is the compassion we show each other as close relatives especially during that time we have lost someone close to us.

She said when it is our time to come over there, there is a small bundle that we carry on our back. In that bundle we carry all the good things we have done for one another including the compassion for our fellow human beings, that has more value; we don't take those material things with us. That's what that old lady talked about.

I am now completing the talk that goes with this.

You are doing Waasigwan good.

He will go where our Anishinaabe go when they are no longer seen here on earth.

See, there are some Anishinaabe that view our ways as inferior and reject it, they are doing wrong.

If an Anishinaabe is sent a different way, he or she does not go anywhere.

Aanjikiing: An Anishinaabe Traditional Funeral

Geget dash gimino-doodawaawaa a'aw Waasigwan.

Gidaa-wii-shawenimigowaag dash ingiw Manidoog.

Mii dash i'iw waabanokeyang, mii iw midaaso-diba'iganek da-ni-maajitaayang.

Mii-go maa minik inwewetooyaan.

Miigwech bizindawiyeg.

You are doing right by Waasigwan.

May the Manidoog have compassion for you for doing this.

Tomorrow we will start at 10 o'clock.

That's all I am going to say.

Thank you for listening to me.

5 AZHIGWA MAAJAA'IND

5.1 Wiindamawindwaa eyaajig imaa da-naabishkaagewaad inow asemaan.

Mii iw akawe da-asisijigaadeg waa-ni-aabajichigaadeg ani-maajaa'iweng, mii dash ge-izhichigeng:

- *Giishpin ininiiwid gaa-ishkwaa-ayaad, booch inow ininiwan oda-ozhiitaa'igoon. Mii-go naasaab a'aw ikwe, booch inow ikwewan oda-ozhiitaa'igoon.*

- *Bashkwegino-makizinan da-biizikoonaa gigizhebaawigadinig apii i'iw giizhigadinig waa-ni-maajaa'ind gaa-ishkwaa-ayaad. Booch i'iw bashkwegin da-aabajichigaadeg izhichigaadeg iniw makizinan.*

- *Mii iw da-agwazhe'ind dabazhish imaa okaading. Mii dash i'iw maamandoogwaason da-aabajichigaadeg, gemaa gaye i'iw waabooyaan gaa-wenda-zaagitood.*

- *Mii dash imaa gendidawizid a'aw asemaa da-achigaazod baabiitawayi'ii inow oninjiing. Mii iw da-giishkizhigaazod a'aw asemaa; niswi dash da-achigaazowan gichinikaang inow oninjiing, naa niizh iwidi namanjinikaang oninjiing.*

- *Mii dash owapii onaawapwan izhichigaadenig a'aw waa-ni-maajaad. Mii imaa bakwebijigaadeg i'iw wiisiniwin gaa-piindigajigaadeg, mii dash imaa achigaadeg biskitenaagaansing. Mii dash imaa biina'igaadeg bezhig i'iw mashkimodensing waa-ni-maajiidood. Giishpin ininiiwid a'aw waa-ni-maajaad,*

5 FUNERAL

5.1 Tell those present to smoke the tobacco.

First all the items that are needed for the funeral are put in place, and this is what will be done:

- *If the deceased is male, then a man will prepare him for his journey. Likewise if the deceased is female, it is only a female who will prepare her for her journey.*

- *Buckskin moccasins are to be placed on the deceased the morning of the funeral. Make sure buckskin is used to make those moccasins.*

- *The body has to be covered from the waist down with a hand-made quilt, or maybe the deceased's favorite blanket.*

- *Plug tobacco is placed in between the fingers. The plug tobacco is cut into pieces; three on the right hand, two on the left.*

- *It is at this time that the lunch is made for the deceased. Bits and pieces of the food that has been brought in are put into the small birch bark basket. The basket containing the food is put into one of the bags that the deceased is taking. If it is a man that is about to go on his journey, it is one of his male relatives that will prepare*

mii inow bezhig ininiiwan besho enawemaajin, mii inow ge-ozisidamaagojin waa-naawapod da-atamaagod imaa biskitenaagaansing. Mii-go gaye giishpin ikwewid waa-ni-aanjikiid, mii inow bezhig inow ikwewan besho enawemaajin da-naadamaagod da-ozisidamaagod ow naawapwaan.

- *Iwedi dash bezhig i'iw mashkimod, mii imaa niiwin gaa-kiishkibijigaadeg i'iw wiigwaas biina'igaadenig miinawaa niiwin ishkodensan. Mookomaanens dash da-atamawaa giishpin ininiiwid waa-ni-maajaa'ind. Mii dash wiin a'aw ikwe waa-ni-maajaa'ind, mii imaa biina'igaadenig ge-aabajitood da-gashkigwaasod.*

- *Mii iw gayat gii-kiizisijigaadeg i'iw wiisiniwin miinawaa gii-paakaakonigaadeg. Mii-go gaye iw wiisiniwin gii-achigaadeg imaa boozikinaaganan gii-kiizisijigaadeg ge-ondanjigewaad ingiw besho enawendaasojig. Mii dash da-maada'oonindwaa besho enawendaasojig dabwaa-agwaaba'amowaad waa-miijiwaad ingiw gaa-pi-naazikaagejig. Mii eta-go imaa Misi-zaaga'iganing ezhichigeng. Mii dash aanind bakaan endanakiijig, mii eta-go bezhig chi-onaagan imaa achigaadeg i'iw wiisiniwin ge-ondanjigewaad ingiw besho enawendaasojig. Mii imaa waakaabiwaad ingiw besho enawendaasojig endazhi-wiisiniwaad.*

Mii dash omaa da-ni-wiindamaageng da-ni-naabishkaageng a'aw asemaa gaa-maada'ookiing.

his lunch. If the deceased is female, it is one of the female
relatives who will prepare her lunch.

- *In the other travel bag four strips of birch bark and four*
  matches are placed. If the deceased is a male, a knife is
  placed in the bag. If the deceased is a woman, a sewing
  kit is placed into the bag.

- *The food is laid out and uncovered. Bowls are placed in*
  front of the casket from which the relatives will eat. The
  bowls will then be passed to the close relatives before
  everyone attending the funeral is served. Mille Lacs is
  the only place that this is done this particular way. For
  those in other communities a platter is placed in front of
  the casket from which the close relatives will eat. The
  close relatives will form a circle around that platter as
  they eat the food.

This is when you will get up and tell everyone to accept the
tobacco on behalf of the Manidoog that was passed out to
them. They can smoke their pipes or take the tobacco to the
fire.

Aanjikiing: An Anishinaabe Traditional Funeral

Mii iw gii-paa-maada'oonigooyeg a'aw asemaa.

Mii imaa da-ni-naabishkaageyeg.

Mii a'aw asemaa ininamawindwaa ingiw Manidoog ge-
onjikaamagadinig-sa a'aw Waasigwan da-ni-
naadamaagoowizid weweni da-ni-giizhiikang da-ni-aanjikiid.

Ishke mii imaa weweni ani-doodawindwaa ingiw Manidoog
ani-niigaaninind a'aw asemaa weweni igo imaa da-ni-
giizhiitaayang waa-ni-izhichigeyang noongom.

Ishke dash imaa ani-giizhi-naabishkaageyang a'aw asemaa, mii
dash imaa da-ni-gaandoweyaan da-ni-wiindamaageyaan
enagimind a'aw asemaa, naa biinish gaye da-ni-dazhindamaan
i'iw wiisiniwin.

Akawe dash omaa weweni naabishkaagedaa a'aw asemaa.

Mii-go maa akawe minik inwewetooyaan.

The tobacco has been passed out to all of you.

It is here that you will accept the tobacco on behalf of the Manidoog.

The tobacco is being handed to the Manidoog and it is from there that Waasigwan will be helped to finish changing worlds.

We are doing good to the Manidoog by putting out tobacco to them first so that we are able to complete what we are doing today.

As we finish accepting the tobacco on behalf of those Manidoog, I will go on to talk about what the tobacco is designated for, and also go on and talk about the food.

So let's accept the tobacco on behalf of those Manidoog in a good way.

This is all I am going to say for the time being.

5.2 Dazhinjigaazod enagimind a'aw asemaa biinish gaye wiisiniwin dazhinjigaadeg.

Mii dash imaa da-ni-dazhinjigaazod enagimind a'aw asemaa biinish gaye da-ni-dazhinjigaadeg i'iw wiisiniwin.

Mii dash gii-maadaabasod a'aw asemaa.

Gaawiin ingoji aanzweyaabasosiin gii-kikinawaadabi'indwaa ingiw Manidoog.

Mii imaa ge-ondiniged a'aw Waasigwan weweni da-ni-naadamaagoowizid da-ni-dagoshimoonod iwidi wenda-onaajiwang i'iw "Gaagige-minawaanigoziwining" ezhiwiinjigaadeg.

Ishke dash a'aw asemaa enagimind, mii imaa weweni gidoodawaanaanig ingiw Manidoog. Geget nebowa imaa ogii-atoonaawaa-sa ge-ni-naadamaagod a'aw Anishinaabe apii enendaagozid da-ni-aanjikiid.

Nebowa imaa gii-achigaadeni ge-ni-naadamaagod a'aw Waasigwan eni-apiichitaad biinish iwidi da-ni dagoshimoonod eni-izhaad a'aw gidinawemaaganinaan gaagwiinawaabaminaagozid omaa akiing.

Ishke dash gaye a'aw asemaa ani-maadaabasod, mii gaye iwidi ge-ni-inaabasod ingiw Manidoog imaa dibikong gaa-tazhinjigaazojig ingiw gaa-pi-zhawenimaajig inow odanishinaabemiwaan gii-miinigoowiziyang o'ow akeyaa da-inakamigiziyang naa-go gaye gii-miinigoowiziyang anishinaabewiyang ge-ni-izhaayang gegoo izhiwebiziyang.

Ishke dash gaye a'aw asemaa enagimind, mii gaye booch gakina imaa enendamowangen gibagosenimaanaanig ingiw

5.2 Tell what the tobacco is designated for and talk for the food.

Now you will talk about where the tobacco goes and about the food.

The tobacco has gone out.

It has gone out to everywhere those Manidoog were seated.

It is from there that Waasigwan will get his help, making sure that he arrives at that beautiful place our people go to that is known as "Land of Everlasting Happiness."

This is what the tobacco is intended for; we are doing those Manidoog good in appreciation for all they put in place to help our people when it is time for Anishinaabe to change worlds.

A lot has been put in place here to help Waasigwan as he goes along on his journey to that beautiful place people go to when they are no longer seen on earth.

As the tobacco goes out, the tobacco will go to those Manidoog who were talked about last night, the ones that took pity on the Anishinaabe people, the ones that gave us this teaching to do this ceremony, and also had given us as Anishinaabe a place to go to when anything happens to us.

The tobacco is also going out in hope that the Manidoog will take pity on the close relatives and watch over them through

Manidoog-sa omaa da-ni-naadamawindwaa zayaagi-
inawendaasojig weweni imaa da-ni-ganawenimigowaad inow
Manidoon omaa epiitakamigiziyang omaa noongom. Ishke
zanagad; gaawiin wenipanasinoon.

Weweni dash oda-ganawenimigowaan inow Manidoon, biinish
gaye da-ni-naadamaagoowiziwaad weweni da-ni-
odaapinamowaad-sa gaa-inaakonigewaad ingiw Manidoog-sa
o'owapii gii-inendaagozid a'aw Waasigwan da-ni-aanjikiid.

Ishke dash gaye ani-maadaabasod a'aw asemaa, gaawiin gaye
niwii-wanenimaasiin a'aw Manidoo epenimod a'aw
Anishinaabe ani-asemaaked wenjida o'ow akeyaa
inakamigiziyang. Mii dash a'aw Giganaan ezhi-wiinind a'aw
Manidoo.

Mii iwidi ge-ni-inaabasod gaye a'aw asemaa. Ishke mii a'aw ge-
ni-naadamaaged giishpin omaa gegoo ani-waniikeyaang ani-
waniwebinigeyaang. Mii a'aw Manidoo ge-ni-nanaa'isidood. Mii
dash a'aw weweni igo a'aw Waasigwan da-ni-wawiinge-
ina'oonwewizid gakina imaa ingiw Manidoog gaa-atoowaad-sa
ge-naadamaagod a'aw Anishinaabe apii enendaagozid da-ni-
aanjikiid.

Biinish gaye omaa ani-dazhimag a'aw asemaa, mii omaa gaye
ani-gaagiizomagwaa ingiw Manidoog giishpin omaa wii-ni-
aanikanootamaageyaan. Gaawiin gaye da-baapinendamaan i'iw
gaa-izhi-ina'oonwewiziyang anishinaabewiyang.

Ishke gaawiin onjida izhiwebizisiin a'aw Anishinaabe, nebowa
gii-waniba'igod i'iw gaa-izhi-miinigod inow Manidoon da-ni-
inwed. Ishke geget gigii-aanooji'igoomin wii-
wayezhimigooyang anishinaabewiyang. Mii eta-go wenji-
izhichigeyaan enendamaan da-ondiniged omaa a'aw
Anishinaabe da-ni-naadamaagoowizid.

the course of the ceremony today; I am sure we are all in the
same frame of mind. It is difficult; it is not easy.

The Manidoog will take care of them, and also help them accept
the decision that those Manidoog made, that it is time for
Waasigwan to change worlds.

As the tobacco goes out, I do not want to forget the Manidoo
that the Anishinaabe rely on when they put tobacco; especially
in this ceremony we are doing. It is the Manidoo that is
referred to as Giganaan.

That tobacco will also go to her. That is the Manidoo that will
help if we should forget something or do something wrong.
That is the Manidoo that will correct it all. So that Waasigwan
is given everything he needs that the Manidoog put here to
help the Anishinaabe when it is time for them to change
worlds.

As I talk for the tobacco I also include asking the Manidoog for
their compassion and understanding when I translate. It is not
out of disrespect for what we have been given as Anishinaabe.

There is a reason that the language has eluded a lot of our
Anishinaabe. The chi-mookomaan made a deliberate effort to
deceive us as Anishinaabe. The only reason I translate is with
the idea of helping our Anishinaabe.

Naa biinish gaye niin iwidi ishkodeng nigii-asaa a'aw indasemaam. Mii ow eni-apagizondamawagig gaye ingiw Manidoog indaa-wii-naadamaagoog omaa-sa ani-ganoodamawag a'aw Waasigwan. Ishke mii ow maamaw-zanagak iko ani-gaagiigidod awiya. Indaa-wii-naadamaagoog dash omaa da-ni-wawiingeziyaan omaa da-ni-naadamawag a'aw Waasigwan.

Ishke dash i'iw mii owapii gaye da-ni-dazhindamaan i'iw wiisiniwin. Gaawiin ingoji apagizonjigaadesinoon o'owapii i'iw wiisiniwin. Akawe igo omaa weweni gida-wiidoopamaanaan epiitawigendang waa-naganinang iko weweni nawajii'ind awiya waasa wii-ni-izhaad.

Ishke dash ingiw akiwenziiyibaneg iko omaa gii-ni-gaagiigidowaad, mii omaa iko gii-ayaangwaamimaawaad iniw zayaagi-inawendaasonijin da-ayaangwaamiziwaad da-ni-odaapinamowaad i'iw wiisiniwin.

Ishke oda-minwendaan da-waabandang weweni ani-odaapinameg i'iw wiisiniwin. Mii-go gaye wiin ge-ni-izhichiged. Ishke odaapinanzig awiya, mii-go gaye wiin gaawiin oda-odaapinanziin. Naa-go gaye gego awiya agwajiing odaa-wii-izhiwidoosiin i'iw wiisiniwin. Naa gaye manaajitoog, gego omaa michisagong daa-wii-pangisinzinoon.

Naa gaye gidaa-wii-mikwendaanaawaa baanimaa gakina awiya omaa gii-ni-giizhiitaad ani-odaapinang i'iw wiisiniwin, mii dash imaa da-ni-gaandoweyaan.

Mii dash gaye owapii dash da-ni-waawiindamawag a'aw Waasigwan gaa-inaabamind a'aw Manidoo apii gii-ozhitood i'iw miikanens, naa gaye da-ni-dazhindamaan i'iw-sa imaa gaa-achigaadeg ani-naadamaagod ani-apiichitaad da-ni-

I also put my own tobacco in the fire. That is the tobacco that I am also sending off to those Manidoog to help me when I am talking for Waasigwan. This is the most difficult talk to do. May they help me be efficient in talking for Waasigwan.

It is at this time that I will talk about the food. The food is not sent anywhere at this time. It is at this time that we will share in a meal with the one that is about to leave us when he so wishes, much like feeding someone before they travel a great distance.

When those old men talked at this point, this is when they encouraged the close relatives to be sure they eat.

Waasigwan will be happy to see you accepting the food in a good way. If someone does not accept the food, he also will not accept the food. Also no one should take the food outside. Handle the food carefully so it does not fall on the floor.

Also you all will want to remember I cannot start talking until everyone has finished accepting the food, it is then that I will continue talking.

That is when I will begin telling Waasigwan what was seen when that Manidoo made that path, and also tell what was put in place to help him as he journeys to that beautiful place called "Land of Everlasting Happiness."

naazikaaged iwidi wenda-onaajiwang "Gaagige-minawaanigoziwining" ezhiwiinjigaadeg.

Mii-go ge-izhi-odaapinamegiban i'iw wiisiniwin.

Mii-go maa akawe minik inwewetooyaan.

You can now accept the food.

That is all I will say for now.

5.3 Wiindamawindwaa eyaajig imaa da-naabishkaagewaad inow asemaan miinawaa.

Mii imaa gii-ni-maada'ookiing a'aw asemaa miinawaa. Ani-giizhi-naabishkaageng, mii dash imaa da-ni-wiindamawind waa-ni-maajaad ge-ni-waabandang eni-apiichitaad da-ni-aanjikiid.

Mii iw gii-paa-maada'oonigooyeg a'aw asemaa.

Mii-go miinawaa da-ni-naabishkaageyeg, mii omaa ge-ondiniged a'aw Waasigwan da-ni-naadamaagoowizid.

Ishke dash imaa ani-giizhi-naabishkaageyeg a'aw asemaa, mii dash imaa da-ni-gaandoweyaan da-ni-waawiindamawag a'aw Waasigwan gaa-inaabamind a'aw Manidoo apii gii-ozhitood i'iw miikanens.

Mii-go maa minik inwewetooyaan.

5.3 Tell those present to smoke the tobacco again.

The tobacco has been passed out again. Once everyone is done smoking the deceased will be told what he will see as he journeys to the other world.

The tobacco has been passed out to all of you.

It is again that you will accept that tobacco on behalf of the Manidoog; it is from there Waasigwan will get his help.

When you are finished accepting the tobacco on behalf of the Manidoog, it is then that I will go on and tell him what was seen when that Manidoo made that path.

That is all I am saying for now.

5.4 Ani-wiindamawind a'aw gaa-ishkwaa-ayaad gaa-inaabamind a'aw Manidoog apii gii-ozhitood i'iw miikanens.

Mii dash imaa da-ni-maajitaang da-ni-wiindamawind a'aw waa-ni-aanjikiid ge-ni-waabandang ani-apiichitaad da-ni-dagoshimoonod iwidi wenda-onaajiwang gii-miinigoowizid a'aw Anishinaabe ge-ni-izhaad gegoo eni-izhiwebizid.

Mii dash gii-maadaabasod a'aw asemaa, gaawiin ingoji aanzweyaabasosiin gii-kikinawaadabi'indwaa ingiw Manidoog.

Mii imaa ge-ondiniged a'aw Waasigwan weweni da-ni-naadamaagoowizid biinish iwidi weweni da-ni-dagoshimoonod iwidi "Gaagige-minawaanigoziwining" ezhi-wiinjigaadeg.

Ishke dash a'aw Anishinaabe geget minochige gaabige gegoo ani-izhiwebizinid inow odinawemaaganan, mii-go gaabige inow asemaan asaad endaso-dibik naa-go gaye omaa nebowa dasing omaa asaad inow asemaan endanakamigiziyang.

Minochige debinaak eni-izhichigesig. Ishke gaawiin debinaak gii-izhichigesiiwag ingiw Manidoog, geget gii-wawiingeziwag inigokwekamig omaa gaa-atoowaad-sa ge-ni-naadamaagod a'aw Anishinaabe apii enendaagozid da-ni-aanjikiid.

Ishke dash mii iw Waasigwan, mii-go omaa wii-ni-maajitaayaan wii-ni-waawiindamoonaan-sa gaa-inaabamind a'aw Manidoo apii gii-ozhitood i'iw miikanens.

Akawe dash omaa gida-ni-waawiindamoon ingiw akiwenziiyibaneg iko gaa-ni-dazhindamowaad omaa gii-ni-ganoonaawaad inow enendaagozinijin iwidi da-ni-izhaanid.

5.4 Tell the deceased what he will see as he makes his journey down that path.

It is at this time that the spirit of the person is told what he will see as he makes that journey to that other world we were given to go to when anything happens to us.

The tobacco has gone out and it will go to every place those Manidoog were seated.

It is from there that Waasigwan will get his help in arriving to the "Land of Everlasting Happiness."

The Anishinaabe does good as soon as something happens to his relative; right away he puts tobacco every night and the tobacco is also offered up several times in this ceremony.

He does good by not doing things half-heartedly. The Manidoog did not do a half-hearted job; they were efficient and put a lot into what will help the Anishinaabe as he changes worlds.

It is here, Waasigwan, that I will begin telling you what was seen when that Manidoo created that path.

It is here I am going to tell you what those old men talked about when they talked to those who are meant to change worlds.

Ishke azhigwa ani-naazikaageyan, gego aabanaabiken.

Naa biinish gaye gego babaamenimaaken ingiw besho
enawemajig, gidaa-inigaa'aag.

Mii-go gaye niin eninaan Waasigwan.

Mii dash owapii da-ni-naangitaayan da-ni-nagadaman i'iw
giwiiyaw.

Mii imaa niiwing da-ni-dakokiiyan.

Mii imaa da-ni-waabandaman i'iw gidishkwaandem.

Ishke dash edawayi'ii i'iw ishkwaandeming gida-waabandaan
i'iw menidoowaadak, mii iw ge-izhinaman inow biizikiganan.

Ishke iwidi akeyaa nebowa a'aw Anishinaabe ezhi-minwiid, mii
iwidi inaabiyan giwaabandaanan, gidinoo'amaagoo gaye, iwidi
biizikiganan etemagakin. Mii-go ezhi-waawaateshkaag inow
biizikiganan.

Gego wiin inow mamooken Waasigwan.

Ishke dash iwidi napaaj akeyaa iw ishkwaandeming inaabiyan,
mii-go gaye iwidi giwaabandaanan, gidinoo'amaagoo gaye,
inow biizikiganan etegin. Biigizawinaagwadoon wiin inow.

Mii dash inow Waasigwan ge-mamooyanin da-ni-biizikaman.

Azhigwa eni-biizikaman, giwaabandaanan ezhi-onaajiwang,
naa gaye gimoozhitoonan ezhi-manidoowaadak inow eni-
naadamaagoowiziyan azhigwa ani-biizikaman.

As you go towards that land over there, do not look back.

Also do not bother with those you are closely related to, you can hurt them.

Waasigwan, this is also what I am saying to you.

It is now that your spirit will up and leave your physical body.

You will take four steps.

It is there you will see your doorway.

On either side of the doorway you will see something in its spiritual form, it will come in the form of clothing in order for you to recognize it.

As you look to the right of the doorway they will point out to you a bundle of clothing. The clothing is bright and shiny.

Do not grab those, Waasigwan.

As you look to the other side of the doorway you will see clothing that they are pointing out to you. The clothing looks dull and drab.

Those are the ones, Waasigwan, you will take and put on.

As soon as you put them on, you will see how nice they really are, and you will feel the spiritual energy in them and will be helped by them.

Ishke gaye gaawiin aanawenjigaadesinoon gaa-izhi-
biizikoonigooyan, onjida ingiw Manidoog imaa ogii-
atoonaawaa-sa da-ni-naadamaagod a'aw Anishinaabe apii
inendaagozid da-ni-aanjikiid.

Mii dash imaa da-ni-zaagi-dakokiiyan i'iw ishkwaandem.

Mii dash imaa da-ni-waabandaman i'iw miikanens a'aw
Wenabozho inow odoozhiman gaa-ozhitoonid.

Ishke iwidi niigaan eko-debaabiyan giwaabandaan izhi-gwayak
inamo i'iw miikanens. Gaawiin gaye ogidaakiiwemagasinoon,
gaawiin gaye niisaakiiwemagasinoon.

Naa biinish gaye imaa dabazhish inaabiyan giwaabandaan
imaa bimikawed a'aw Anishinaabe gaa-ni-niigaaniid.
Bashkwegino-makizinan ogii-piizikaanaawaan.

Mii iwidi bezhigwaning izhikawewaad iwidi akeyaa izhi-
naazikaageyan, gaawiin awiya biijikawesiin.

Gego babaamendangen i'iw Waasigwan, eta-go mikwendan
ezhi-onaajiwang iwidi eni-izhaayan.

Naa gaye booch weweni da-ni-odaapinaman, da-ni-mamooyan-
sa gaa-inaakonigewaad ingiw Manidoog-sa owapii gii-
inendaagoziyan da-ni-aanjikiiyan.

Ishke dash mii i'iw da-ni-maada'adooyan i'iw miikanens.

Ginwenzh gida-ni-bimose, gida-ni-minwaabishin gaye, aaniish
naa a'aw Manidoo gaa-ozhitood i'iw miikanens.

Ishke dash iwidi Waasigwan megwaa ani-bimi-ayaayan, mii
iwidi da-ni-waabandaman dibishkoo gii-miskokamigaa.

This is not discounting the clothing your relatives have put on you, those have been put there for a reason to help our people when it is time to change worlds.

It is at that time you will step through that doorway.

It is then that you will see that path that Wenabozho's nephew made.

As far as you can look ahead you will see that the path goes straight. It does not go uphill or downhill.

And as you look down you will see the footprints of the Anishinaabe that have gone on before you. They were wearing buckskin moccasins.

Their footprints only go in one direction, the direction you are going; there are none coming back.

Do not let that bother you, Waasigwan, just remember how beautiful that place is that you are going to.

And you will also have to accept and take the decision those Manidoog made, that it was time for you to change worlds at this time.

Then you will start going down that path.

You will be walking a long time and it will look beautiful, after all it was a Manidoo that made that path.

Waasigwan, as you are going along that path you will look down and the ground will look as if it is reddish.

Mii imaa da-ni-noogitaayan da-ni-ojijiingwanabiyan da-ni-mawinzoyan dash inow ode'iminan ezhi-wiinjigaadegin.

Azhigwa nigaapoonoyan inow ode'iminan gida-moozhitoonan ezhi-manidoowaadak inow. Mii-go dibishkoo gii-koshkwaabaawe ge-inendaman

Mii dash i'iw aabiding ani-bakwenigaadeg ani-naazhaabaawemagak i'iw gaa-kagwaadagi'igoyan.

Naa gaye aanind gimamaag ishkweyaang gidapaginaag da-wii-manezisigwaa ingiw gidinawemaaganag.

Gaa-te-nigaapoonoyan inow ode'iminan, mii-go miinawaa da-ni-maada'adooyan i'iw miikanens.

Ginwenzh gida-ni-bimose.

Ishke dash iwidi azhigwa maa minik ani-dagoshimoonoyan, mii iwidi da-wii-ni-noogitaayan da-ni-anwebiyan.

Ishke gaye mii iwidi da-ni-boodaweyan gaye.

Ishke geget weweni gigii-toodaagoog ingiw gidinawemaaganag, weweni imaa wiigwaas gigii-atamaagoo naa-go gaye inow ishkodensan.

Naa-go gaye mii imaa da-ni-nawajiiyan ginawapwaan. Ishke gaye weweni gigii-toodaagoog ingiw gidinawemaaganag imaa ogii-atoonaawaa i'iw ginawapwaan.

This is where you will stop, squat down and pick the strawberries.

As you begin to eat those strawberries you will begin to feel the spiritual energy in them. It will startle you as if you were splashed with water.

One portion of that which bothered you is removed and washes down, leaving your spirit.

You will grab some of those strawberries and throw them behind, remembering your relatives so they are not lacking spiritual nourishment.

As soon as you have your fill of those strawberries, you will again start walking down that path.

You will be walking for a long time.

After you have been traveling on that path for some time, you will want to stop and rest.

It is then that you will also make your fire.

Your relatives did you good by putting birch bark and matches in there for you.

And at that time you will eat your lunch. Your relatives also did you good by putting a lunch for you also.

Ishke dash i'iw azhigwa gaa-te-anwebiyan, mii-go da-ni-naazikaman i'iw miikanens a'aw Manidoo gaa-ozhitood da-ni-maada'adooyan.

Ginwenzh miinawaa gida-ni-bimose.

Ishke dash iwidi maa minik azhigwa ani-dagoshimoonoyan gida-odisaa a'aw Manidoo iwidi gaa-asind da-ganawendang i'iw miikanens.

Ishke weweni gaye gigii-toodaagoog ingiw gidinawemaaganag.

Weweni imaa asemaa gigii-atamaagoo. Mii ow gimamaa a'aw asemaa ininamawad a'aw Manidoo.

Naa aapidek waa-inwewetood ezhi-minwendang-sa weweni ani-doodawad ani-biindaakoonad, naa gaye gizhawenimitaag naa gaye ginanaakomig-sa imaa ani-wiindamawad iwidi ezhi-naazikaageyan.

Mii-go ezhinoo'ang i'iw miikanens a'aw Wenabozho inow odoozhiman gaa-ozhitoonid.

Mii-go miinawaa da-ni-maada'adooyan.

Mii dash i'iw azhigwa ginwenzh ani-bimi-ayaayan i'iw miikanens megwaa iwidi ani-bimi-ayaayan, mii imaa da-ni-waabandaman imaa dibishkoo gii-ozhaawashkokamigaa.

Once you have rested you will approach the path that Manidoo made and begin walking.

You will be walking a long long time.

Once you have traveled a great distance down that path you will run into a Manidoo that has been placed there to watch over that path.

Your relatives also did you good.

They put tobacco in there for you. You take a piece of that tobacco and hand it to the Manidoo.

He makes noises to show his appreciation for you treating him respectfully by giving him tobacco. He listens to you with compassion and he answers you when you tell him where you are going.

He points at that path that Wenabozho's nephew made, allowing you to go further.

And again you will start walking down that path.

Once you have been down that road for quite some time, you will come upon something that looks bluish on the ground.

Mii imaa da-ni-noogitaayan.

Mii dash owapii da-ni-misabiyan.

Mii dash owapii da-ni-mawinzoyan inow miinan ezhi-wiinjigaadegin.

Azhigwa nigaapoonoyan inow miinan, gimoozhitoonan ezhi-manidoowaadak inow.

Mii dash i'iw niizhing gii-ni-maajaamagak ani-naazhaabaawemagak i'iw gaa-kagwaadagi'igoyan.

Naa gaye aanind gimamaag, ishkweyaang gidapaginaag da-wii-manezisigwaa ingiw gidinawemaaganag.

Gaa-te-nigaapoonoyan inow miinan, mii-go da-ni-maada'adooyan i'iw miikanens.

Ginwenzh miinawaa da-ni-bimoseyan.

Azhigwa dash Waasigwan, ginwenzh gaa-ni-bima'adooyan i'iw miikanens, mii iwidi booch da-wii-ni-noogitaayan miinawaa da-ni-anwebiyan.

Mii-go gaye da-ni-boodaweyan, naa-go gaye da-ni-nawajiiyan i'iw ginawapwaan.

Gaa-te-anwebiyan, mii-go iw miinawaa da-ni-naazikaman i'iw miikanens a'aw Manidoo gaa-ozhitood da-ni-maada'adooyan miinawaa.

Ginwenzh gida-ni-bimose.

It is there you will stop.

It is at that time you will kneel down.

It is at that time you will pick blueberries.

Once you have ingested those blueberries, you will feel the spiritual energy within them.

It is then that the second portion of what has bothered you washes off.

You will also take some of them and throw them behind so that your relatives are not lacking.

Once you have had your fill of those blueberries, you will continue to walk down that path.

You will be walking a long time again.

Once you have been walking down that path for a long time, Waasigwan, you will want to stop and rest again.

Once again you will make your fire and eat your lunch.

After you have had enough rest, you will approach that path once again that the Manidoo made and continue on.

You will be walking for a long long time.

Ishke dash iwidi megwaa ani-bimoseyan, mii iwidi da-odisad a'aw Manidoo gaye wiin iwidi gaa-asind da-ganawendang i'iw miikanens.

Ishke geget gimino-doodaagoog ingiw gidinawemaaganag imaa weweni asemaa gii-atamaagooyan, mii iw gaa-ikidowaad ingiw akiwenziiyibaneg, "Gaawiin odaa-gashkitoosiin awas da-ni-izhaapan awiya ani-gigishkawaasig ani-bimiwinaasig inow odasemaan."

Mii ow gimamaa a'aw asemaa ininamawad a'aw Manidoo.

Mii dash imaa bagidinik awas da-ni-izhaayan.

Ishke dash gaye Waasigwan giwii-wiindamoon.

Ishke giwaabandaan i'iw eshkam gida-ni-gizhiikaa gida-ni-gizhiimaajii. Mii imaa wenjikaamagak-sa ingiw Manidoog gaa-atoowaad imaa miikanensing ge-naadamaagod a'aw Anishinaabe apii inendaagozid da-ni-aanjikiid.

Naa gaye nigii-wiindamaagoo da-wanendanziwaan imaa da-ni-dazhindamaan ayaapii bakemo i'iw miikanens.

Gego awiya gidaa-wii-wayezhimigosiin Waasigwan. Mii-go izhi-aabiji-bima'adoon i'iw miikanens a'aw Manidoo gaa-ozhitood.

Ishke dash a'aw Waasigwan azhigwa ani-maada'adooyan i'iw miikanens ginwenzh gida-ni-bimose miinawaa. Mii dash iwidi megwaa ani-bimi-ayaayan, mii imaa da-ni-waabandaman dibishkoo-go gii-miskogoodemagad gegoo.

Mii imaa da-ni-noogitaayan

Now as you are walking along you will come upon a Manidoo.
He too has been put there to watch over that path.

Your relatives did you good by sending tobacco along with you.
What the old men said was that, "Nobody could go further
without having their tobacco with them and on them."

You take the tobacco and hand it to the Manidoo.

Then he allows you to go further down that path.

Waasigwan, I also want to tell you:

You will see that you are able to move faster and move better.
It is a result of what the Manidoog had put along the path to
help the Anishinaabe when it is time to change worlds.

I was also told not to forget to talk about those side roads on
that path.

Do not let anyone deceive you, Waasigwan, into taking one of
those side roads. Just continue on that path that the Manidoo
made.

Waasigwan, as you continue down that path, you will walk a
long time again. As you are going along, it is there you will see
something reddish hanging there.

This is where you will stop.

Mii dash da-ni-ojijiingwanigaabawiyan.

Mii dash imaa da-ni-mawinzoyan ingiw miskominag ezhi-wiinjigaazojig.

Azhigwa nigaapoonoyan ingiw miskominag, gida-ni-moozhi'aag ezhi-manidoowaadiziwaad ingiw. Mii-go imaa giiwenh gii-segaabaawe ge-inendaman.

Mii dash i'iw nising gii-ni-maajaamagak, gii-ni-naazhaabaawemagak i'iw gaa-kagwaadagi'igoyan.

Naa gaye aanind ishkweyaang gidapaginaag da-wii-manezisigwaa ingiw gidinawemaaganag.

Gaa-te-nigaapoonoyan ingiw miskominag, mii-go miinawaa da-ni-maada'adooyan i'iw miikanens.

Ginwenzh gida-ni-bimose.

Ishke iwidi azhigwa maa minik ani-dagoshimoonoyan, mii-go miinawaa iwidi booch da-ni-noogitaayan da-ni-anwebiyan.

Mii-go gaye da-ni-boodaweyan naa-go gaye da-ni-nawajiiyan ginawapwaan.

Gaa-te-anwebiyan, mii-go da-ni-naazikaman i'iw miikanens da-ni-maada'adooyan i'iw miinawaa.

Ginwenzh miinawaa gida-ni-bimose.

Ishke dash iwidi megwaa ani-bimi-ayaayan, mii iwidi da-odisad a'aw Manidoo gaye wiin iwidi gaa-asind da-ganawendang i'iw miikanens.

It is then that you will bend over.

It is there that you will pick what is known as raspberries.

Once you have ingested those raspberries you will feel how spiritually powerful they are. It is said here that you will think that you have been splashed with water.

It is at that time the third portion of what has bothered you washes off.

You also throw some behind so that your relatives are not lacking in spiritual nourishment.

After you have had your fill of raspberries, you will continue down that path once again.

You will be walking a long time.

Once you have gone so far, you will stop again to rest.

You will make your fire and eat your lunch again.

Once you have rested enough, then you will continue down that path again.

You will be walking for a long time again.

While you are going along, you will come upon a Manidoo who also has been put there to watch over that path.

Mii ow ani-mamad a'aw asemaa ininamawad a'aw Manidoo.

Mii dash imaa bagidinik awas da-ni-izhaayan ani-biindigeyan wenjida meshkawaamagak gaa-achigaadeg da-ni-naadamaagod a'aw Anishinaabe apii inendaagozid da-ni-aanjikiid.

Ishke dash a'aw Waasigwan azhigwa ginwenzh ani-bimi-ayaayan i'iw miikanens, megwaa iwidi bimi-ayaayan, mii imaa da-ni-niibawiyan, mii imaa ishpiming inaabiyan dibishkoo gii-miskogoodemagad gegoo.

Mii imaa da-ni-noogigaabawiyan.

Mii dash imaa apii da-ni-mawinzoyan ingiw bagesaanag ezhi-wiinjigaazojig.

Azhigwa ani-baapaashkamadwaa ingiw bagesaanag, gida-moozhi'aag gaye wiinawaa izhi-manidoowaadiziwaad ingiw.

Mii dash owapii gakina eni-maajaamagak, eni-naazhaabaawemagak i'iw gaa-kagwaadagi'igoyan.

Mii-sa azhigwa bakaan da-inenindizoyan, mii wiin da-gweki-manidoowiyan.

Naa gaye aanind gimamaag ishkweyaang gida-apaginaag da-manezisigwaa ingiw gidinawemaaganag.

Gaa-te-nigaapoonoyan ingiw bagesaanag, mii-go ani-maada'adooyan i'iw miikanens da-ni-naazikaageyan miinawaa.

Ginwenzh miinawaa gida-ni-bimose.

You take your tobacco and hand it to that Manidoo.

This is where he allows you go further down that path and where that which is most especially powerful has been placed that will help our people when it is time to change worlds.

Waasigwan, once you have gone down that path for a long time, while you are going along, you will be standing there. As you look above you, it will look as if something reddish is hanging.

It is there where you will stop and stand.

It is then that you will be picking plums, as they are called.

As you bite through those plums you will feel how powerful they are.

It is at that time all that has bothered you washes off.

It is then that you will begin to think differently about yourself; it is like you are turning into a Manidoo.

And you will take some of them and throw them behind, remembering your relatives.

Once you have had your fill of those plums, you will continue down that path heading towards that place our people go.

You will be walking a long time again.

Ishke dash iwidi azhigwa ginwenzh ani-bimi-ayaayan i'iw miikanens, mii iwidi booch miinawaa da-wii-ni-noogitaayan da-ni-anwebiyan.

Mii-go gaye da-ni-boodaweyan, naa gaye da-ni-nawajiiyan i'iw ginawapwaan.

Gaa-te-anwebiyan, mii-go iw da-ni-naazikaman i'iw miikanens miinawaa da-ni-maada'adooyan.

Ginwenzh miinawaa gida-ni-bimose.

Ishke dash iwidi megwaa ani-bimi-ayaayan, mii iwidi da-odisad a'aw Manidoo gaye wiin iwidi gaa-asind da-ganawendang i'iw miikanens.

Mii ow gimamaa a'aw asemaa gaa-atamaagooyan ininamawad a'aw Manidoo.

Mii dash imaa bagidinik awas da-ni-izhaayan.

Ishke dash Waasigwan azhigwa ginwenzh ani-bima'adooyan i'iw miikanens, megwaa iwidi ani-bimi-ayaayan mii iwidi da-ni-oditaman i'iw ziibi iwidi eyaamagak.

Geget gizhiijiwan i'iw ziibi.

Gaawiin odaa-gashkitoosiin awiya imaa da-ni-aazhogepan.

Ishke dash imaa dabazhish inaabiyan imaa ziibiing, giwaabamaa zhingishing a'aw Manidoo.

Gaawiin bizaanishinziin, mii-go enaabogod epidenig i'iw ziibi.

As you have been going down that path for a long time, you will also have to stop and rest again.

You will also make your fire and eat your lunch.

Once you have rested, you will approach that path and start walking down that path.

You will be walking a long time again.

As you go along you will come upon a Manidoo that has been put there to watch over that path also.

You will take your tobacco placed there for you and hand it to the Manidoo.

It is then that he allows you to go further.

Waasigwan, after you have been walking down that path for a long time, as you go along you will come upon that river that exists over there.

That river is really swift.

Nobody would be able to cross it.

As you look down into the river, you will see a Manidoo lying there.

He is not lying still, he is moving like that river.

Ishke dash a'aw Waasigwan ezhi-naadamaagoowizid a'aw Anishinaabe geyaabi iwidi ani-aabaji'aad inow asemaan.

Mii ow gimamaa a'aw asemaa atamawad a'aw Manidoo.

Mii dash imaa izhi-bizaanishing bagidinik-sa imaa weweni ani-akwaandaweyan ani-aazhogeyan i'iw ziibi.

Azhigwa ani-aazhogeyan i'iw ziibi, mii dash iwidi besho ani-dagoshimoonoyan iwidi ayaawaad gidinawemaaganinaanig.

Gidebaabandaan iwidi oodetoowaad naa gaye gidebaabandaan iwidi i'iw chi-wiigiwaam bemidesing.

Ishke dash Waasigwan gaye giwii-wiindamoon, mii-ko enind awiya azhigwa iwidi inendaagozid da-ni-izhaad, gego aabanaabiken azhigwa iwidi eni-naazikaageyan. Ishke ishkweyaang inaabiyamban gidaa-gii-waabamaa ezhi-zeginaagozid a'aw Manidoo gaa-pagidinik imaa da-aazhogeyan i'iw ziibi.

Ishke awanjish iwidi gii-ni-aazhoged awiya, gaawiin odaa-gashkitoosiin da-bi-azhegiiwed.

Gego Waasigwan babaamendangen i'iw, eta-go mikwendan izhi-onaajiwang iwidi eni-izhaayan naa gaye booch weweni da-ni-odaapinaman da-ni-mamooyan-sa gaa-inaakonigewaad ingiw Manidoog-sa owapii gii-inendaagoziyan da-ni-aanjikiiyan.

Ishke dash mii owapii da-ni-aabajichigaadeg i'iw Manidoo-giigidowin imaa gaa-achigaadeg da-ni-maajaa'igoyan.

See, Waasigwan, how Anishinaabe are helped when they use their tobacco even over there.

You will take your tobacco and place it there for that Manidoo.

It is there that he lies still and allows you to climb over his back and cross that river safely.

Once you have crossed that river, you are getting close to that place where our relatives are.

You can see that community over there and you can see that big wigwam that sits sideways over there.

Waasigwan, I am going to tell you what is usually told to someone who is making that journey when it is their time. They are told not to look back. If you were to look back at that time you would have seen how ferocious-looking that Manidoo was that allowed you to cross that river.

Once a person has crossed that river, he is not able to come back.

Don't let that bother you, Waasigwan, just remember only how beautiful it is where you are going, and that you must accept and take the decision those Manidoo have made that it is your time to change worlds.

It is at this time that the Manidoo's song that has been put here will be used to send you on this journey.

Ishke dash mii imaa da-ni-aabajichigaazod gaye a'aw zhiishiigwan.

Ishke a'aw wawiingezi ani-ganoodamawaad inow odanishinaabeman.

Naa gaye biinish gaawiin ingoji da-naaweweshinziin enabiwaad ingiw Manidoog.

Ishke ani-aabajichigaazod a'aw zhiishiigwan, Waasigwan, mii-go ge-ni-inwewemagak imaa ani-bimi-ayaayan i'iw miikanens.

Gida-aabiji-gikenimigoog ingiw Manidoog aaniindi ani-bimi-ayaayan imaa miikanensing, geget weweni gida-ganawenimigoog.

Mii-go maa akawe minik inwewetooyaan.

It is here that the rattle will be used.

The rattle is efficient in speaking for his Anishinaabe.

And it is also heard everywhere those Manidoog sit.

When the rattle is used, that is the sound that will be heard as you go down that path.

Those Manidoog will always know where you are at and will take good care of you.

This is all I am saying for the time being.

5.5. I'iw manidoo-giigidowin da-ni-aabajichigaadeg da-ni-maajaa'igod a'aw gaa-ishkwaa-ayaad.

Mii imaa da-ni-aabajichigaadeg i'iw manidoo-giigidowin ge-ni-maajaa'igod a'aw waa-ni-aanjikiid.

Mii imaa nitam ena'igaadeg:

Maajaayan maajaayane

Maajaayan maajaayane

Maajaayan maajaayane

Maajaayan maajaayane

Maajaayan maajaayane

Maajaayan maajaayane

Weweni maajaayane

Maajaayan maajaayane

Maajaayan maajaayane

Maajaayan maajaayane

5.5. The song that is used to send the spirit of the deceased down that path.

This is the song that is used to send off the spirit of that person that is about to change worlds.

First half of the song:

You are leaving, you are leaving

You are leaving, you are leaving

You are leaving, you are leaving

You are leaving, you are leaving

You are leaving, you are leaving

You are leaving, you are leaving

You are leaving in a good way

You are leaving, you are leaving

You are leaving, you are leaving

You are leaving, you are leaving

Mii dash imaa ena'igaadeg ani-giizhikigaadeg i'iw nagamon:

Maajaayan maajaayane

Maajaayan maajaayane

Maajaayan maajaayane

Maajaayan maajaayane

Aazhawoode izhaan maajaayane

Maajaayan maajaayane

Maajaayan maajaayane

Maajaayan maajaayane

Words for second half of the song:

You are leaving, you are leaving

You are leaving, you are leaving

You are leaving, you are leaving

You are leaving, you are leaving

Crawl across the river as you are leaving

You are leaving, you are leaving

You are leaving, you are leaving

You are leaving, you are leaving

5.6 Omaa nawaj ani-gaagiigidong ani-wiindamawind gaa-ishkwaa-ayaad da-ni-giizhiikang da-ni-aanjikiid.

Mii dash imaa ani-giizhiikigaadeg i'iw gaagiigidowin gaa-achigaadeg omaa ani-wiindamawind a'aw ge-ni-waabandang ani-apiichitaad biinish iwidi da-ni-dagoshimoonod ayaawaad gidinawemaaganinaanig.

Ishke dash a'aw Waasigwan, geget ingiw Manidoog ogii-shawenimaawaan inow odanishinaabemiwaan.

Inigokwekamig imaa gaa-achigaadeg ani-naadamaagoyan ani-apiichitaayan iwidi weweni da-ni-giizhiikaman da-ni-aanjikiiyan.

Gaawiin gegoo gida-gotanziin. Weweni gida-ganawenimigoog ingiw Manidoog.

Ishke dash omaa gii-wiindamoonaan gii-ni-aazhogeyan iw ziibi, mii iwidi debaabandaman ayaawaad gidinawemaaganinaanig.

Mii-go da-ni-maada'adooyan miinawaa i'iw miikanens a'aw Wenabozho inow odoozhiman gaa-ozhitoonid da-ni-naazikaageyan.

Ishke dash iwidi besho ani-dagoshimoonoyan, gida-waabamaag nebowa ingiw akiwenziiyag gibi-nagishkaagoog.

Mii-go ge-bi-izhi-noondaagoziwaad miinawaa zhiishiigwanan gakina da-bi-madweshimaawaad. Gego dash babaamenimaaken.

5.6 Finish telling the deceased the final part of the journey.

It is here where you finish the talk that has been put here telling the spirit of the deceased what he will see as he approaches that place where our people go when they leave this world and completes his journey to where our relatives are.

Waasigwan, the Manidoog definitely had compassion for their Anishinaabe.

They put a lot there that will help you as you go along, finishing your move to change worlds.

There is nothing that you will be scared of. The Manidoog will take care of you as you make your journey.

I have told you that as you cross that river over there, you will see that community over there, where our people are.

You will continue on that path again that Wenabozho's nephew made, approaching that community over there.

As you get closer to where our people are, you will see a lot of old men coming to meet you.

You will hear them singing and the sound of their rattles. Do not let this bother you.

Mii-go izhi-gwayak iwidi ani-izhaan. Azhigwa iwidi ani-dagoshimoonoyan Waasigwan, mii iwidi da-ni-biindiganigooyan i'iw chi-wiigiwaam iwidi bemidesing.

Ishke imaa ani-biindigeyan geget gida-ni-minwaabishin.

Mii-go imaa eni-agoojinowaad ingiw Miigisag biindig, naa gaye Manidoo imaa ayaa biindig weweni gida-ganawenimig, naa gaye inow odooshkaabewisiman odayaawaan.

Ishke mii imaa niiyo-giizhik da-ganawenimigooyan.

Ishke dash ingiw akiwenziiyibaneg gaa-ikidowaad bakaan inendaagwadini ogiizhigadomiwaa iwidi.

Mii-go aabiding bapazangwaabiyang, mii iw ekwaamagadinig wiinawaa ogiizhigadomiwaa.

Azhigwa gaa-niiyo-giizhigadinig wiinawaa ogiizhigadomiwaa, mii dash a'aw Manidoo imaa eyaad imaa wiigiwaaming ezhi-wiindamawaad inow odooshkaabewisiman "Daga baa-waawiindamaw imaa eyaajig bi-dagoshinini bezhig inow odinawemaaganiwaan."

Mii dash geget baa-waawiindamaagewaad.

Mii dash owapii Waasigwan da-ni-bagidinigooyan i'iw chi-wiigiwaam.

Mii dash imaa da-ni-waabamadwaa gidinawemaaganag gaa-minjinaweziyan gaye giin.

Mii-go ezhi-biijibatoowaad naa-go ezhi-noondaagoziwaad ezhi-minwendamowaad-sa waabandamowaad i'iw weweni iwidi ani-dagoshimoonoyan.

Waasigwan, just keep going and go directly to that place where our people are. When you get there they will take you into this huge wigwam that sits sideways.

As you go in, you will see how beautiful it is in there.

You will see those shells used in our Midewiwin ceremonies hanging inside that wigwam, and there is a Manidoo in there that will take care of you, and he also has his helpers.

It is there that they will keep you four days.

The old men said that their days are much different up there than they are here on earth.

The length of their days is equivalent to a blink of our eye.

Once their four days have passed, the Manidoo in the wigwam tells his helpers, "Go out and tell the people here that a relative of theirs has arrived."

And that is what they do, they go out and tell everyone.

It is at that time they release you from that big wigwam.

It is at that time you will see your relatives that you also had a difficult time seeing leave.

They come running and you can hear how happy they are to see you have arrived over there safely.

Ishke dash ingiw gidinawemaaganag omaa mii inow asemaan da-asaawaad naa gaye i'iw wiisiniwin.

Mii dash iwidi bijiinag apagizonjigaadeg naa-go gaye jaagizigaadeg. Azhigwa iwidi ani-dagoshimoonagak, mii iwidi da-ni-wiidoopamadwaa ingiw gidinawemaaganag iwidi eyaajig.

Eni-giizhi-wiidoopamadwaa, mii dash iwidi da-ni-wiij'ayaawadwaa.

Ishke dash aw Waasigwan geget onaajiwan iwidi eni-izhaayan.

Gaawiin gegoo wiiyagasenh iwidi ayaamagasinoon ezhi-onaajiwang.

Naa-go gaye gakina gaa-izhi-ina'oonwewizid a'aw Anishinaabe inakamigizid, mii iw enakamigiziwaad iwidi.

Geget ow minawaanigwad, gaawiin gegoo gida-wanishkwe'igosiin.

Ishke mii imaa ani-giizhiikamaan ow gaagiigidowin omaa gaa-achigaadeg.

Ishke moozhag nigii-nanaandomaa a'aw Manidoo omaa giishpin gegoo gii-waniikeyaang gii-waniwebinigeyaang, mii a'aw Manidoo ge-ni-nanaa'isidood.

Mii dash i'iw Waasigwan, mii iwidi ge-danenimikwaa ingiw Manidoog biinish gaye gidinawemaaganag.

Mii-go maa minik inwewetooyaan.

116

Then your relatives here will put tobacco and food.

It is then that the food is finally sent over there and is also burned. When it arrives over there, you will share in that meal with your relatives who are over there.

Once you have finished eating with them, it is then you will go on to live with them.

Waasigwan, it is a beautiful place that you are going to.

It is so beautiful up there that there is no dust.

And everything that the Anishinaabe have been given ceremonial-wise, that is what happens over there.

It is especially happy over there; nothing will bother you.

I have completed the talk that has been put here.

I called on that Manidoo several times in case we may have forgotten or left something out; that is the Manidoo that will correct any mistakes.

Waasigwan, the Manidoog and your relatives will consider you being over there.

That is all I will say for the time being.

5.7 Waabamind awiya.

Mii dash apii da-ni-waabamind, mii imaa da-ni-wiindamawindwaa ge-izhichigewaad azhigwa ani-waabamind a'aw waa-ni-maajaad.

Mii dash owapii ge-izhi-waabamegiban.

Ayaangwaamizig sanaa gego imaa nibi gishkiinzhigowaang gijaanzhiwaang daa-wii-pangisinzinoon azhigwa imaa ani-waabameg.

Giishpin i'iw izhiwebak, mii-go da-ni-gagwaadagitood ani-maajaad naa gaye da-ni-awanibiisaamagadinig imaa ani-bimi-ayaad imaa miikanensing.

Naa gaye mii-ko ingiw akiwenziiyibaneg ogii-tazhindaanaawaa, a'aw ikwe gegishkawaad miinawaa ekawaabamaad oniijaanisan, gaawiin odaa-bi-waabamaasiin awiya, naa gaye ingiw bebiiwizhiiwijig abinoojiinyag gaawiin omaa odaa-bi-waabamaasiwaawaan awiya.

Naa gaye gidaa-wii-mikwendaanaawaa da-giizikameg inow gidooshkiinzhigokaaniwaan.

Ayaangwaamizig sanaa.

Mii-go maa inwewetooyaan.

5.7 Viewing

This is the viewing; instructions are given out on what to do when viewing.

It is at this time you will view him.

Be careful; don't let water from you eyes or nose fall on the body when you are viewing him.

If that happens, he will have a difficult time leaving and there will be a mist as he goes down that path.

Our old men of the past said that women who were expecting were not allowed to view the body, and also young children were not allowed to view the body.

And also remember to take off your glasses when you are viewing.

Be careful now.

That is all I am saying.

6 GAA-TAGOSHIMOONOD

6.1 Wiindamawindwaa eyaajig imaa da-naabishkaagewaad inow asemaan.

Mii iw iwidi gii-ni-dagoshimoonod gaa-ni-maajaa'ind iwidi ayaawaad gidinawemaaganinaanig. Mii dash akawe asemaa maada'ookiing. Mii omaa da-ni-wiindamawindwaa da-naabishkaagewaad inow asemaan. Ani-giizhiitaang mii dash imaa nawaj ani-gaagiigidong ani-dazhimind a'aw asemaa miinawaa i'iw wiisiniwin.

Mii dash owapii ani-aabajichigaadeg i'iw biskitenaagaans, wiisiniwin imaa achigaadeg imaa biinjina miinawaa waa-minikweng miinawaa a'aw asemaa. Mii dash izhi-jaagizigaadeg ani-niindaa'iweng da-ni-izhaamagak gaa-izhaad a'aw gaa-ishkwaa-ayaad.

Mii iw gii-paa-maada'oonigooyeg a'aw asemaa.

Mii dash imaa da-ni-naabishkaageyeg weweni.

Ishke dash mii ow wenji-achigaazod a'aw asemaa miinawaa i'iw wiisiniwin. Mii iw noongom iwidi gii-ni-dagoshimoonod a'aw Waasigwan "Gaagige-minawaanigoziwining" ezhi-wiinjigaadeg.

Eni-giizhi-naabishkaageyang, mii imaa da-ni-dazhimag a'aw asemaa enagimind miinawaa i'iw wiisiniwin da-ni-dazhindamaan.

Akawe dash ani-naabishkaagedaa a'aw asemaa.

6 POST-FUNERAL FEAST

6.1 Tell those present to smoke the tobacco.

The spirit of the one who has left has arrived where our relatives are. First the tobacco has been passed out. They are told to light up or put the tobacco in the fire. When they are done smoking, more talking will be done to address the tobacco and the food that is being offered up.

A small birch bark basket is placed in the fire, and in the little basket we put bits and pieces of the food brought into the feast, along with a drop of the drink being served and a pinch of tobacco. And this food is being sent to the one who has arrived over there where our relatives are. He will share in that meal with his relatives over there.

The tobacco has been passed out to you.

You are going to accept the tobacco on behalf of the Manidoog in a good way.

See, this is why we are putting tobacco and food. It is at this time that Waasigwan arrives over there at that place called "Land of Everlasting Happiness."

When we get done accepting the tobacco, I will talk about the purpose of the tobacco and also the food.

Let's take in that tobacco for the Manidoog.

6.2 Dazhinjigaazod enagimind a'aw asemaa biinish gaye wiisiniwin dazhinjigaadeg

Mii dash imaa ani-dazhinjigaazod a'aw asemaa miinawaa i'iw wiisiniwin naandaa'iweng. Mii imaa ani-niindaa'ind a'aw iwidi gaa-ni-dagoshimoonod biinish gaye odinawemaaganan gaa-odisaajin.

Mii gii-ni-maadaabasod a'aw asemaa.

Mii iwidi eni-inaabasod gakina enabiwaad ingiw Manidoog, mii imaa ani-miigwechiwi'indwaa inigokwekamig gaa-achigaadeg gaa-naadamaagod a'aw Waasigwan gaa-ni-apiichitaad biinish iwidi weweni gii-ni-dagoshimoonod gii-ni-giizhiikang gii-ni-aanjikiid.

Naa-go gaye gimiigwechiwi'aanaanig ingiw Manidoog gii-miinigoowizid a'aw Anishinaabe da-niindaa'aad i'iw wiisiniwin inow odinawemaaganan iwidi eyaanijin.

Miinawaa ani-maadaabasod a'aw asemaa, mii iwidi ge-ni-inaabasod a'aw Manidoo iwidi eyaad genawenimaad gidinawemaaganinaanan miinawaa inow odooshkaabewisiman.

Ishke dash azhigwa iwidi Waasigwan gii-ni-dagoshimoonod, mii iw iwidi gii-piindiganind a'aw chi-wiigiwaam iwidi bemidesing.

Mii iw iwidi niiyo-giizhik da-ganawenjigaazod a'aw Waasigwan. Bakaan inendaagwadini ogiizhigadomiwaa iwidi, ingiw akiwenziiyibaneg gii-ikidowag. Mii aabiding bapazangwaabiyang, mii iw ekwaamagadinig o'ow ogiizhigadomiwaa.

6.2 Tell what the tobacco is designated for and talk for the food

At this time the tobacco is being talked about and also the food that is being sent over there. The food is sent to the one that has arrived over there and also to the relatives that he has a reunion with.

The tobacco has gone out.

It went to where all the Manidoog sit. We are thanking them for all that has been put in place that helped Waasigwan as he went along, eventually arriving over there completing the process of changing worlds.

We are also thanking the Manidoog for the ability to send food over to where our relatives are.

And the tobacco also goes to the Manidoo that takes care of our relatives over there and to his helpers.

As Waasigwan arrives over there, they take him into this huge wigwam that sits sideways.

They will keep Waasigwan there for four days. Those old men say that their days are different than ours over there. The length of their day is equivalent the blink of an eye.

Azhigwa gaa-niiyo-giizhigadinig wiinawaa ogiizhigadomiwaa iwidi, mii dash a'aw Manidoo eyaad imaa wiigiwaaming ezhi-wiindamawaad inow odooshkaabewisiman, "Daga baa-wiindamaw omaa eyaajig, bi-dagoshinini bezhig inow odinawemaaganiwaan."

Mii dash geget baa-waawiindamaagewaad.

Ishke dash o'ow wiisiniwin omaa etemagak, mii iwidi epagizondamaan miinawaa i'iw wiisiniwin gaa-chaagizigaadeg, mii iw iwidi ezhaamagak gaye.

Mii dash iwidi da-ni-wiidoopamaad inow odinawemaaganan gaa-odisaajin Waasigwan.

Nebowa ayaadogenan odinawemaaganan iwidi.

Gaawiin gaye gimakandamawaasiwaanaan i'iw wiisiniwin. Baanimaa gakina gii-tebisewendamowaad, mii iw da-gwiinawaabandamowaad i'iw wiisiniwin. Waasa izhaamagad i'iw wiisiniwin iwidi.

Miinawaa gaawiin bimaadiziwin ginandodamawaasiwaanaanig. Mii-go ezhi-inigaawendamowaad giishpin awiya inendang i'iw akeyaa.

Mii eta-go weweni doodawind a'aw Waasigwan miinawaa inow odinawemaaganan gaa-odisaajin.

Mii dash gaye a'aw asemaa enagimind, ingiw besho enawendaasojig oda-wii-ni-naadamaagowaan inow Manidoon da-ni-odaapinamowaad weweni gaa-inaakonigenid inow Manidoon-sa owapii gii-inendaagozid a'aw Waasigwan da-ni-aanjikiid.

124

As soon as their four days have passed, the Manidoo in that wigwam tells his helpers, "Go tell the people that a relative of theirs has arrived"

And then they go and tell the people.

The food before us I am sending over there and also the food that was burnt in the fire arrives over there.

It is then that Waasigwan will eat with all his relatives that he has met up with.

There must be a lot of his relatives over there.

We are not taking food from him. It not until they are all content that the food is gone. A small amount of food goes a long way in that world.

We are not asking our relatives for life. If someone thinks that way, our relatives would feel bad.

We are only doing good to Waasigwan and the relatives that he saw upon his arrival.

The tobacco is also being put to help the close relatives to accept the decision of the Manidoog that it was time for Waasigwan to change worlds.

Mii dash gaye iwidi ge-ni-inaabasod a'aw asemaa a'aw
Giganaan. Ishke giishpin gegoo omaa waniikeyaan
waniwebinigeyaan, mii a'aw Manidoo ge-ni-nanaa'isidood.

Ishke dash ayaapii wiisiniwin gidaa-atamawaawaa Waasigwan
da-ni-mikwenimeg.

Ishke giishpin a'aw Anishinaabe ezhichigesig, obi-
wiindamaagoon inow odinawemaaganan eyaanijin iwidi da-
mikwenimindwaa. Obawaanaawaan iko.

Ishke dash gida-wii-shawenimigowaag ingiw Manidoog
weweni ani-giizhiikameg o'ow akeyaa gaa-izhi-
gikinoo'amaagoowiziyang da-ni-izhichigeyang
anishinaabewiyang.

Mii-go iw ge-izhi-naabishkaageyegiban i'iw wiisiniwin.

Mii iw.

That tobacco will also go to the Moon. If I should forget something or omit something, she will correct it.

You can put food every so often, remembering Waasigwan.

See, if the Anishinaabe do not do that, their relatives over there will come to tell them that they want to be remembered. They usually dream about them.

May the Manidoog have compassion for you all for completing this ceremony as we have been taught to do as Anishinaabe.

Now you can eat the food that will go to Waasigwan and his relatives over there.

That's it.

7 MIKWENIMIND AWIYA

7.1 Wiindamawindwaa eyaajig imaa da-naabishkaagewaad inow asemaan.

Azhigwa i'iw bezhig i'iw gikinoonowin gaa-pimisemagak, mii owapii aanind a'aw Anishinaabe niindaa'aad i'iw wiisiniwin miinawaa ge-aabajitoonid inow odinawemaaganan gaa-wani'aajin. Asemaa gii-maada'ookiim mii dash imaa apii ani-wiindamawindwaa da-ni-naabishkaagewaad inow asemaan.

Mii iw gii-paa-ininamaagooyeg a'aw asemaa miinawaa i'iw wiisiniwin gii-kiizisijigaadeg, biinish gaye i'iw naandaa'ind a'aw mekwenimind.

Ishke dash a'aw asemaa, wiisiniwin, miinawaa bagijigan wenji-achigaadeg, mii iw bezhig i'iw gikinoonowin gii-pimisemagadinig owapii gaa-inendaagozid a'aw Waasigwan da-ni-aanjikiid.

Weweni dash omaa odoodaagoon inow odinawemaaganan ani-mikwenimigod. Weweni dash da-naabishkaageyeg a'aw asemaa.

Ani-giizhiitaayeg, mii imaa da-ni-dazhimag enagimind a'aw asemaa biinish gaye gakina omaa naandaa'iweng.

Mii-go maa akawe minik ani-izhi-gaagiigidoyaan.

7 ONE-YEAR MEMORIAL FEAST

7.1 Tell those present to smoke the tobacco.

After a year has passed since their relative has passed on, some Anishinaabe put food and other items remembering their relative that has passed on. The tobacco has been passed out; at this time everyone is given permission to smoke or put their tobacco in the fire.

Everyone has been handed tobacco and the food has been laid out, and also those things that will be sent to the one who is being remembered.

The reason the tobacco, the food, and the gifts are going to be sent out is because it has been a year since Waasigwan was meant to change worlds.

His relatives are doing him good by remembering him. Take the tobacco in, in a good way.

When you are done smoking I will go on to talk about the tobacco and all that has been placed here that will be sent out.

That is all I will say for now.

7.2 Dazhinjigaazod enagimind a'aw asemaa biinish gaye wiisiniwin dazhinjigaadeg.

Mii dash omaa ani-apagizonjigaazod a'aw asemaa miinawaa i'iw wiisiniwin apagizonjigaadeg iwidi ayaawaad gidinawemaaganinaanig. Mii iwidi ani-dagoshimoonagak, mii dash ezhi-wiindamawind a'aw mekwenimind, mii dash imaa gakina inow odinawemaaganan da-wiidoopamigod.

Mii iwidi enikaad a'aw asemaa ani-bagamimaasod iwidi gakina enabiwaad ingiw Manidoog. Ishke dash enagimind a'aw asemaa, mii omaa ani-miigwechiwi'indwaa ingiw Manidoog gii-miinigoowizid a'aw Anishinaabe-sa da-niindaa'aad i'iw wiisiniwin miinawaa ge-ni-aabajitoonid odinawemaaganan iwidi gaa-izhaanijin eni-izhaad gidinawemaaganinaan gaagwiinawaabaminaagozid omaa akiing.

Gaawiin ingikenimaasiin aw bekaanizid bemaadizid da-gii-miinigoowizipan i'iw da-izhichiged. Geget ingiw Manidoog ogii-shawenimaawaan inow odanishinaabemiwaan gii-miinaawaad ow akeyaa da-ni-izhichigenid.

Mii-go gaye a'aw asemaa da-ni-bagamimaasod iwidi a'aw Manidoo eyaad genawenimaad inow gidinawemaaganinaanan gaa-aanjikiinijin. Mii a'aw Manidoo weweni ge-ni-odaapinaad inow asemaan. Biinish gaye mii iwidi ani-biindaakoonindwaa inow odooshkaabewisiman azhigwa ani-bagamimaasod iwidi a'aw asemaa.

Mii dash a'aw Manidoo iwidi eyaad izhi-wiindamawaad inow odooshkaabewisiman da-o-wiindamawaawaad-sa a'aw mekwenimind a'aw Waasigwan.

7.2 Tell what the tobacco is designated for and talk for the food.

The tobacco is sent out and the food is sent over to where our relatives go. As the food arrives over there, the one who is being remembered is told and then he shares a meal with all his relatives over there.

The tobacco has arrived to where those Manidoog sit. The tobacco is being sent to them to thank the Manidoog for giving Anishinaabe the ability to send food and other items to their relatives who have gone to that place our relatives go when they are no longer seen here on earth.

I do not know of any other people that have been given the ability to do this. The Manidoog really had compassion for the Anishinaabe by giving them this ceremony.

The tobacco is also arriving to the Manidoo over there that takes care of our relatives who have already changed worlds. That Manidoo will take the tobacco in a good way. The tobacco is also being given to his helpers as it arrives over there.

And then that Manidoo over there tells his helpers to tell Waasigwan that he is being remembered.

Mii-go gaye gakina odinawemaaganan gaa-odisaajin biinish gaa-odisigojin da-bi-wiijiiwigod a'aw Waasigwan. Mii dash iwidi ani-apagizondamaan o'ow wiisiniwin omaa gaa-achigaadeg. Mii dash iwidi da-ni-wiidoopamaad a'aw Waasigwan inow odinawemaaganan iwidi eyaanijin.

Ishke nebowa ayaadogenan inow odinawemaaganan iwidi. Gaawiin gaye makandamawaasiin i'iw wiisiniwin a'aw Waasigwan baanimaa gakina gaa-tebisewendamowaad, mii iw da-gwiinawaabandamowaad i'iw wiisiniwin.

Gaawiin gaye bimaadiziwin omisawendamaagosiin inow odinawemaaganan imaa eyaanijin. Mii-go ezhi-inigaawendamowaad iwidi eyaajig, giishpin i'iw akeyaa inendang awiya.

Mii eta-go omaa weweni ani-doodaagod inow odinawemaaganan omaa eyaanijin ani-mikwenimigod Waasigwan o'owapii bezhig i'iw gikinoonowin gii-pimisemagak i'iwapii gii-inenimigod inow Manidoon da-aanjikiid.

Ishke dash inow odayi'iimaanan miinawaa i'iw ge-ni-aabajitood awiya omaa gaa-achigaadegin, mii gaye iwidi ani-apagizondamaan ani-niindaa'ind a'aw Waasigwan.

Mii ow "Giiweniged" ezhinikaadang a'aw Anishinaabe.

Ishke dash ani-giizhi-naabishkaageng i'iw wiisiniwin, mii dash imaa da-ni-maada'ookiing inow bagijiganan da-ni-naabishkaageyeg minik ayaayeg omaa.

Also his relatives that he has met up with and that met up with him will come with Waasigwan. It is over there that I am sending the food that has been placed here. And Waasigwan will share in a meal with all of his relatives that are over there.

There must be a lot of his relatives over there. Waasigwan will not be deprived of any of the food. The food will not be gone until they are all content.

His relatives here are not asking that those who have passed on be given life. If someone were to think this way, the relatives over there would feel bad.

His relatives here are only trying to do good to Waasigwan by remembering him, especially since it has been a year since it was meant for him to change worlds.

I am also sending the items of clothing and all the miscellaneous useful items to Waasigwan.

This is what the Anishinaabe call "Giiweniged."

After we get done eating, the items from the bundle will be passed out to all of you here to accept on behalf of Waasigwan.

Mii dash iwidi weweni da-ni-dagoshimoonagak. Weweni manaajitoog omaa waa-paa-maada'oonigooyeg. Wiikwajitoog wewiib da-biizikameg inow odayi'iimaanan gaa-paa-maamiinigooyegin, naa wewiib da-aabajitooyeg inow aabajichiganan gaa-paa-maamiinigooyegin.

Ishke minokanziweg inow biizikiganan, gidaa-miinaawaa awiya ge-minokang. Mii dash ow weweni da-ni-dagoshimoonagak inow naandaa'iwengin.

Ishke dash gaye ani-maadaabasod a'aw asemaa, mii iwidi ge-ni-inaabasod a'aw Manidoo epenimod a'aw Anishinaabe ani-asemaaked. Mii dash a'aw Giganaan ezhi-wiinind. Mii a'aw ge-ni-nanaa'isidood imaa giishpin gegoo ani-waniikeyaan ani-waniwebinigeyaan. Weweni dash igo da-aawang i'iw akeyaa ezhi-bagosendamang omaa okwi'idiyang.

Ishke dash omaa gidaa-wii-shawendaagozim omaa izhi-mino-doodaweg a'aw gidinawemaaganiwaa gaa-ni-aanjikiid. Geget minwaabishinowidogenag gimino-waabamigoominaadog i'iw akeyaa ezhi-minochigeyeg omaa noongom ani-ayaangwaamitooyeg i'iw akeyaa gaa-izhi-gikinoo'amaagoowiziyang anishinaabewiyang da-ni-izhichigeyang. Gidaa-wii-shawenimigowaag dash ingiw Manidoog.

Mii-go maa minik ezhi-gaagiigidoyaan.

That way it will all arrive over there to him. Treat the items you have been given with respect. Make an effort to wear those items that you have been given as soon as possible and make an effort to use those miscellaneous items that you have also been given.

If you cannot fit the clothing, you can give them to someone who can fit them. That way those things that are being sent over to Waasigwan will arrive there properly.

The tobacco is also going out to that Manidoo the Anishinaabe rely on when they offer up their tobacco. That is the Manidoo that is named Giganaan. She is the one that will correct it if I were to forget something or make an error. That way everything will be accomplished that we wish to do through this ceremony.

May you be shown compassion by those Manidoog for doing what is good for your relative that has gone on and changed worlds. The Manidoog must really enjoy and like what they see in you all for doing such a good thing today, continuing on this ceremony that we were given as Anishinaabe. May those Manidoog offer their compassion to you all as a result.

That is all I want to say for now.

Ikidowinan / Ojibwe-English Glossary

Key to Ojibwe Word Class Codes

adv	adverb
na	animate noun
nad	dependent animate noun
name pers	personal name
name place	place name
ni	inanimate noun
nid	dependent inanimate noun
pc	particle
pron dem	demonstrative pronoun
pron indf	indefinite pronoun
pron inter	interrogative pronoun
pron per	personal pronoun
pv	preverb
vai	animate intransitive verb
vai2	class 2 animate intransitive verb
vai+o	animate intransitive verb with object
vii	inanimate intransitive verb
vta	transitive animate verb
vti	class 1 transitive inanimate verb
vti2	class 2 transitive inanimate verb
vti3	class 3 transitive inanimate verb
vti4	class 4 transitive inanimate verb

Other Abbreviations

h/	an animate object: him or her or it (animate); his or hers
s/he	an animate subject: she or he or it (animate)
h/self	himself or herself
pl	plural

abi *vai* s/he is at home, is in a certain place, sits in a certain place

abinoojiinh *na* child

abinoojiiyens *na* infant

abiitaw *vta* sit up with h/, hold a wake for h/

achigaade *vii* it is put in a certain place (by someone), "they" put it in a certain place

achigaazo *vai* s/he is put in a certain place (by someone); "they" put h/ in a certain palce

agaasatemagad *vii* it is small (as a room or house)

agaawaa *adv* hardly, barely

agana *adv* not to the least, less

agindan *vti* read it, count it

agokajigaade *vii* it is attached (by someone); "they" attach it

agoojin *vai* s/he hangs; s/he is in the sky (e.g., a star, the sun, the moon)

agwajiing *adv* outside, outdoors

agwazhe' *vta* cover h/ with blankets

a'aw *pron dem* that; *animate singular demonstrative; also* **aw**

akawaabam *vta* expect h/

akawe *adv* first (in time sequence), first of all, for now

akeyaa *adv* in the direction of, that way

aki *ni* earth, land, ground, country

akiwenzii *na* old man

ako- *pv* since, a certain length, as long as, as far as

akwaamagad *vii* it is a certain length, is so long; it is a certain height, is so tall

akwaandawe *vai* s/he climbs up

Amikogaabaw *name pers* Larry Smallwood

Amikogaabawiikwe *name pers* Julie Shingobe

amo /amw-/ *vta* eat h/

anama'e-maajaa' *vta* hold a Christian funeral for h/

anang *na* star

anaamakamig *adv* underground

anaamayi'ii *adv* under something

ani- *pv* going away, going along, in progress, on the way, coming up in time; also **ni-**

anishinaabe *na* Ojibwe, person, human, Indian (in contrast to non-Indians)

anishinaabe-maajaa'iwe *vai* s/he holds an Anishinaabe funeral

anishinaabewi *vai* s/he is Ojibwe, human, Indian (in contrast to non-Indians)

anokiitan *vti* work at it

anooj *adv* various, all kinds

anoozh /anooN-/ *vta* ask h/ to do something, hire h/, give an order to h/, commission h/

anwebi *vai* s/he rests

apagidan *vti* throw it

apagizh /apagiN-/ *vta* throw h/

apagizondamaw *vta* sent (it) to h/ (by voice)

apagizondan *vti* send it (by voice)

apagizonjigaade *vii* it is sent (by voice); "they" send it (by voice)

apagizonjigaazo *vai* s/he is sent (by voice); "they" send h/ (by voice)

apa'iwe *vai* s/he runs away from people to a certain place

apane *adv* always, all the time, continually

apenimo *vta* s/he relies on something, s/he depends on something

apii *adv* when, then, at the time

apiichitaa *vai* s/he is engaged in an activity to a certain extent, s/he is so far along in an activity

apiitakamigizi *vai* s/he is engaged in an event to a certain extent, s/he is or goes so far along doing something

apiitawigendam *vai* s/he does something at h/ own leisure

apiitendan *vti* value it to a certain extent, appreciate it

apiitendaagwad *vii* it is valued to a certain extent, to a certain rank

apiitenim *vta* be proud of h/ to a certain extent, feel about h/ to a certain extent

apiitenindizo *vai* s/he is proud of h/self to a certain extent, s/he has self-esteem

asemaa *na* tobacco

asemaakaw *vta* make an offering of tobacco to h/

asemaake *vai* s/he makes a tobacco offering

asham *vta* feed (it) to h/

ashangewigamig *ni* welfare office

ashi /aS-/ *vta* put h/ in a certain place

asigishin *vai* h/ [tobacco] collects together

asigisijigaade *vii* it is collected (by someone); "they" collect it

atamaw *vta* put something in a certain place for h/

ataagewigamig *ni* casino

ate *vii* it is in a certain place

atemagad *vii* it is in a certain place

atoon *vti2* put it in a certain place

aw *pron dem* that; *animate singular demonstrative; also* **a'aw**

awanibiisaamagad *vii* it is misty

awanjish *adv* even though, once

awas *pc* go further

awenen *pron inter* who; *animate interrogative*

awesiinh *na* wild animal

awiya *pron indf* somebody, anybody; *animate indefinite*

ayaa *vai* s/he is (in a certain place); *with a lexical preverb* s/he is in a certain state; *with a directional preverb* s/he moves in a certain way

ayaamagad *vii* it is (in a certain place); *with a lexical preverb* it is in a certain state; *with a directional preverb* it moves in a certain way

ayaan /ayaam-/ *vti4* have it, own it

ayaangwaami- *pv* carefully, cautiously

ayaangwaamim *vta* encourage h/, warn h/, caution h/

ayaangwaamitoon *vti2* carefully do it, cautiously do it

ayaangwaamizi *vai* s/he is careful, s/he is cautious

ayaapii *adv* every once in a while, every so often

ayaaw *vta* have h/, own h/

ayi'ii *pausal pro* that thing

azhe- *pv* go back

azhegiiwe *vai* s/he goes or comes back, s/he returns

azhigwa *adv* now, at this time, already, then

aabajichigan *ni* useful item, tool

aabajichigaade *vii* it is used (by someone), "they" use it

aabajichigaazo *vai* s/he is used (by someone), "they" use h/

aabaji' *vta* use h/

aabajitoon *vti2* use it

aabanaabi *vai* s/he turns and looks back

aabiding *adv* once, at one time

aabiji- *pv* continually, constantly

aabita-diba'igan *adv* half an hour

aana- *pv* in vain, without result

aanawendamaw *vta* dislike something of h/, rejects something of h/, finds something of h/ unsatisfactory or inferior

aanawendan *vti* dislike it, reject it, discount it, find it unsatisfactory or inferior

aanawenim *vta* dislike h/, reject h/, find h/ unsatisfactory or inferior

aanawenindizo *vai* s/he finds h/self unsatisfactory or inferior

aanawenjigaade *vii* it is disliked, rejected, found unsatisfactory or inferior (by someone), "they" dislike, reject, find it unsatisfactory or inferior

aanikanootamaw *vta* translate (it) for h/

aanikanootamaage *vai* s/he translates to people

aanind *adv* some

aaningodinong *adv* sometimes, occasionally

aaniin *adv* how?, why?, in what way?

aaniin igo *adv* whatever

aaniindi *adv* where?

aaniindi-go *adv* wherever

aaniish naa *adv* after all, well now; you see

aanjikii *vai* s/he changes worlds

aanjitoon *vti2* change it, make it over

aano-go *adv* anyhow, although, despite, but; *also* **aanawi-go**

aanoodizi *vai* s/he desires, s/he is determined

aanooji' *vta* desires h/, goes after h/

aanzikan *vti* change it (something on the foot or body, e.g., clothes)

aanzweyaabaso *vai* h/ smoke goes everywhere

aapideg *adv* without a doubt, certainly

aapiji *adv* very, quite

aawan *vii* it is a certain thing

aazhaweyaatig *na* cross

aazhawoode *vai* s/he crawls across

aazhita *adv* in return

aazhoge *vai* s/he goes across, crosses

babaa- *pv* going about

babaamaadizi *vai* s/he lives about, s/he travels about

babaamendan *vti* be bothered by it

babaamenim *vta* be bothered by h/

babaamibatoo *vai* s/he runs about

babaamidaabii'iwetamaw *vta* drive h/about

babaamiziwin *ni* business; organization; responsibility

babiiwaabaminaagozi *vai* s/he looks small; **bebiiwaabaminaagozijig awesiinyag** little animals

babiiwizhiiwi *vai* s/he is tiny

bagamimaaso *vai* h/ smoke arrives

bagesaan *na* plum

bagidenim *vta* let h/ go from your mind

bagidin *vta* set h/ down, offer h/, release h/, let h/ go, allow h/

bagijigan *ni* offering

bagosendam *vai2* wish, hope

bagosendan *vti* wish for it, hope for it

bagosenim *vta* wish for h/, hope for h/

bagwaj *adv* in the wilderness, out in the woods

Bagwajiwinini *name pers* The Big Man in the Woods (a Manidoo that lives in the woods and appears as a man)

bakaan *adv* different

bakaanad *vii* it is different

bakaanizi *vai* s/he is different

bakemo *vii* it goes off to the side (as a road or trail)

bakwenigaade *vii* a portion of it is removed (by someone); "they" remove a portion of it

banaajitoon *vti2* spoil it, damage it

bangishimo *vai* the sun sets

bangisin *vii* it falls

bangiiwagizi *vai* there is a little bit of h/; *plural* there are few of them

bapazangwaabi *vai* s/he blinks h/ eyes

bashkwegino-makizin *ni* buckskin moccasin

bawaazh /bawaaN-/ *vta* dream of h/

bazigwii *vai* s/he stands up

baa- *pv* going about

baabii'o *vai* s/he keeps waiting

baabiitawayi'ii *adv* inbetween

baabiitawi- *pv* in layers; advance through stages

baabiiwaabikishin *vai* s/he (rock) lies on the earth; **Bayaabiiwaabikishingig omaa akiing** the rocks on this earth

baakaakonigaade *vii* it is opened (as something stick- or wood-like, e.g., a casket) (by someone), "they" open it

baanimaa *adv* later, after awhile

baapaashkam *vta* bite and burst h/

baapinendan *vti* be disrespectful to it

baataashin *vai* s/he gets stuck

bebezhig *adv* one-by-one

besho *adv* near, close

bezhig *adv* one

bezhigwaning *adv* one place, in one place

bi- *pv* this way, here, hither

bibizhaagii *vai* s/he lives in a certain place

biboon *vii* it is winter

bijiinag *adv* after awhile, recently, just now

bima'adoo *vai* s/he follows a path along

bimaadizi *vai* s/he lives, s/he is alive

bimaadiziwin *ni* life

bimi- *pv* along, going along, going by, going past, on the way

bimidesin *vii* it sits sideways

bimikawe *vai* s/he leaves tracks going along

biminizha'an *vti* chase it along, pursue it

bimisemagad *vii* it (time) goes along, passes

bimiwanaan *ni* bundle, pack

bimiwidoon *vti2* carry it along, take it along; carry it on, conduct it

bimiwizh /**bimiwiN-**/ *vta* carry h/ along, take h/ along

bimose *vai* s/he walks along

bimoondan *vti* carry it along on your back

Binesiwag *na-pl* Thunder-Beings

biskitenaagaans *ni* small folded birch bark basket

bitaakoshkan *vti* bump into it

bizaanishin *vai* s/he lies still

bizindaw *vta* listen to h/

Biidaanakwad *name pers* John Nichols

biigizawinaagwad *vii* it is dull or drab in color

biijibatoo *vai* s/he runs here

biijikawe *vai* s/he comes leaving tracks

biina'igaade *vii* it is put inside (by someone), "they" put it inside

biindaakoozh /**biindaakooN-**/ *vta* make an offering of tobacco to h/

biindig *adv* inside

biindigadoon *vti2* bring it inside, take it inside

biindigajigaade *vii* it is being brought inside (by someone), "they" are bringing it inside

biindigazh /**biindigaN-**/ *vta* bring h/ inside, take h/ inside

biindige *vai* s/he enters, s/he goes inside, s/he comes inside

biingeyenim *vta* s/he is astonished about h/

biinish *adv* until, up to; continuing on

biinish gaye *adv* and also

biinjayi'ii *adv* inside it

biinji- *pv* inside

biinjina *adv* inside the body

biizikan *vti* wear it, have it on (e.g., clothes), put it on (e.g., clothes)

biizikaw *vta* wear h/, have h/ on (e.g., clothes), put h/ on (e.g., clothes)

biizikigan *ni* item of clothing

biizikoozh /**biizikooN**/ *vta* dress h/, put clothes on h/

booch *adv* it is necessary, it is certain, you have to

boodawe *vai* s/he builds a fire

boonitoon *vti2* leave it alone, quit it

boozikinaagan *ni* bowl

Bwaani-dewe'igan *na* ceremonial drum, big drum; Sioux drum

chi- *pv* big, great; *also* **gichi-**

chi-mookomaan *na* whiteman

Chi-oshkaabewis *name pers* Big Messenger (Sun); Manidoo

da- *pv* will; *future prefix in independent verbs*

da- *pv* will, that, so that, in order to; *future prefix in unchanged conjunct;* also **ji-**

dabazhish *adv* low, down low

daga *pc* please! come on!

dagoshimoonagad *vii* it arrives

dagoshimoono *vai* s/he arrives

dagoshimoono' *vta* get h/ to h/ destination

dagoshin *vai* s/he arrives

dagosijigaade *vii* it is added to something (by someone); "they" add it to something

dakokii *vai* step

danakamigad *vii* it (an event) takes place, happens in a certain place

danakamigizi *vai* s/he has an event in a certain place

danakii *vai* s/he lives in a certain place

danenim *vta* think h/ to be in a certain place, expect h/ to be in a certain place

dapine *vai* s/he suffers in a certain place, s/he dies in a certain place

dash *adv* and

dasing *adv* a certain number of times, so many times

dazhi- *pv* in a certain place, of a certain place, there

dazhim *vta* talk about h/, discuss h/

dazhindan *vti* talk about it, discuss it

dazhinjigaade *vii* it is talked, about, discussed (by someone), "they" talk about, discuss it

dazhinjigaazo *vai* s/he talked about, discussed (by someone), "they" talk about, discuss h/

dazhitaa *vai* s/he spends time, works in a certain place

dazhiikan *vti* work on it, be involved with it, handle it

dazhiikaw *vta* work on h/, be involved with h/, handle h/

daa *vai* s/he lives in a certain place; **endaashaan** where I live, my home

daa- *pv* would, could, should, can, might

de- *pv* sufficient, suitable, enough

debaabandan *vti* have it in sight, see it at a distance

debaabi *vai* s/he can see in the distance

debinaak *adv* carelessly, half-heartedly

debisewendam *vai2* s/he is content, feels satisfied

debitaw *vta* be able to hear h/, hear h/ at a distance, catch the sound of h/

debwetan *vti* believe it (something heard)

debweyendan *vti* believe in it

dedebinawe *adv* by oneself, inherently, actual, biological

diba'amaw *vta* pay h/ for (it), pay (it) for h/

diba'igaade *vii* it is paid (by someone); "they" pay it

dibaadodan *vti* tell of it, talk about it

dibaajimo *vai* s/he tells, tells a story

dibendan *vti* control it, be the master of it, own it, earn it

dibiki-giizis *na* moon

dibikong *adv* last night

dibishkoo *adv* just like, even, equal, direct

doodan *vti* do something to it

doodaw *vta* do something to h/

doodaadizo *vai* s/he does something to h/self

edawayi'ii *adv* on both sides

eko-nising *adv* the second time

eko-niiwing *adv* the fourth time

eko-niizhing *adv* the second time

endaso-dibik *adv* every night

endaso-giizhik *adv* every day

eshkam *adv* gradually, more and more, less and less

eta *adv* only

gaganoodamaage *vai* s/he talks for people

gaganoozh *vta* talk to h/, have a conversation with h/

gagaanzom *vta* encourage h/, urge h/, persuade h/

gagiibaadenim *vta* think h/ is foolish

gagiikim *vta* teach h/, preach to h/

gagwaadagi' *vta* bother h/, make h/ suffer

gagwaadagitoo *vai* s/he has a difficult time

gagwaadagi'idiwag /gagwaadagi'idi-/ *vai* they make things difficult for each other

gagwedwe *vai* s/he asks questions, s/he inquires

gagwejim *vta* ask h/

gakina *adv* all

ganabaj *adv* one thinks that, maybe

ganawaabandan *vti* look at it, watch it

ganawendamaage *vai* s/he takes care of things for people

ganawendan *vti* take care of it, watch over it

ganawenim *vta* take care of h/, watch over h/

ganawenjigaazo *vai* s/he is taken care of, is kept

ganoodamaw *vta* speak for h/

ganoodamaage *vai* s/he speaks for people

ganoozh /ganooN-/ *vta* address h/, speak to h/

gashkapijigaade *vii* it is wrapped and tied in a bundle (by someone); "they" wrap and tie it in a bundle

gashkapijigaazo *vai* s/he is wrapped and tied in a bundle (by someone); "they" wrap and tie h/ in a bundle

gashkigwaaso *vai* s/he sews

gashki'ewizi *vai* s/he is able to do something, is capable

gashkitoon *vti2* be able to do it, succeed at it, manage it

gayat *adv* formerly, previously, some time ago

gaye *adv* as for, also, too, and

Gaa-biboonike *name pers* Manidoo in the Snow (Snow)

Gaa-zhiigwanaabikokaag *name place* Hinckley, Minnesota

gaabige *adv* immediately, quickly, right away

Gaagige-minawaanigoziwining *name place* Land of Everlasting Happiness

gaagiigido *vai* s/he talks, s/he speaks

gaagiigidowin *ni* speech, talk

gaagiiwozhitoo *vai* s/he wanders about

gaagiizom *vta* ask for compassion from h/, appease h

gaagwiinawaabaminaagozi *vai* s/he is unable to be seen, is no longer seen; *reduplication of* **gwiinawaabaminaagozi**

gaagwiinawendamaw *vta* miss it (something of h/), feel the absence of it (something of h/) for a length of time; *reduplication of* **gwiinawendamaw**

gaagwiinawendan *vti* miss, feel the absence of it for a length of time; *reduplication of* **gwiinawendan**

gaagwiinawenim *vta* miss h/, feel the absence of h/ for a length of time; *reduplication of* **gwiinawenim**

gaakiizhiikan *vti* finish with it; *reduplication of* **giizhiikan**

gaakiizhiitaa *vai* s/he finishes work, s/he finishes tasks; *reduplication of* **giizhiitaa**

gaandowe *vai* s/he goes on talking, continues on speaking

gaawiin *adv* no, not

gaawiin mashi *adv* not yet

gaawiin memwech *adv* it is not necessary

gaazh /gaaN-/ *vta* hide h/

ge- *pv* future tense preverb under initial change

gegapii *adv* after a while, eventually, finally

geget *adv* sure, indeed, certainly, really

gego *adv* don't

gegoo *pron indf* something, anything; *inanimate indefinite*

gemaa *adv* or, or maybe

Gete-bwaan *name pers* Jimmy Jackson

geyaabi *adv* still, yet

gibishkaw *vta* block h/

gichi-aya'aawi *vai* s/he is an elder

gichinik *ni* right hand

gidimaagizi *vai* s/he is poor, pitiful

gigabi *vai+o* sit with (it)

Giganaan *name pers* our grandmother, the Moon; Manidoo

gigishkaw *vta* bear h/ on one's body, be pregnant with h/

gigizheb *adv* in the morning

gigizhebaawagad *vii* it is morning; **endaso-gigizhebaawagak** every
    morning

gijaanzhiwaan /-jaanzh-/ *nid* your (plural) noses

gikendamookaazo *vai* s/he pretends to know

gikendan *vti* know it

gikenim *vta* know h/, know of h/

gikina'amaw *vta* forbid h/ to, warn h/ against (it); *reduplication of*
    gina'amaw

gikinawaabam *vta* copy h/

gikinawaadabi' *vta* seat h/ in a designated spot

gikinoo'amaw *vta* teach it to h/

gikinoo'amaage *vai* s/he teaches, instructs

gikinoo'amaagozi *vai* s/he goes to school

gikinoo'amaagoowizi *vai* s/he is taught

gikinoonowin *ni* year

Gimishoomisinaanig *na pl* Our Grandfathers (The rocks on this earth);
    Drums

gina'amaw *vta* forbid h/ to, warn h/ against (it)

gindidawizi *vai* s/he is whole; **gendidawizid a'aw asemaa** plug tobacco

ginigisijigaade *vii* it is mixed in (by someone); "they" mix it in

giningwanisinaan /-ningwanis-/ *nad* our (inclusive) cross-nephew (male's sister's son or female's brother's son)

giniigaaniiminaan /-niigaaniim-/ *nid* our (inclusive) future; **giniigaaniiminaang** in our future

ginwenzh *adv* for a long time

gishkiinzhigowaan /-shiinzhigw-/ *nid* your (plural) eyes

giwiiyaw /-wiiyaw-/ *nid* your body

gizhiijiwan *vii* it flows swiftly

gizhiikaa *vai* s/he goes fast

gizhiimaajii *vai* s/he moves fast

gizhiiwe *vai* s/he speaks loud, speaks up

giziingwe'on *ni* towel

giziingwe'oons *ni* wash cloth

gii- *pv* was, did; *past tense*

giigidowin *ni* speech, song (text)

giigoonh *na* fish

giin *pron per* you (singular); *second person singular pronoun*

giinawaa *pron per* you (plural); *second person plural pronoun*

giinawind *pron per* we, us; *first person inclusive plural pronoun including the person or persons spoken to with the speaker*

giishkibijigaade *vii* it is torn into pieces (by someone), "they" tear it into pieces

giishkigaadezh /gishkigaadezhw-/ *vta* cut off h/ leg(s)

giishkininjiizh /giishkininjiizhw-/ *vta* cut off h/ finger(s)

giishkizhigaazo *vai* s/he is cut (by someone); "they" cut h/

giishpin *adv* if

giiwe *vai* s/he goes home, s/he returns

giiwedin *ni* north wind, north

giiwenh *pc* so the story goes; so it is said

giiwenige *vai* s/he gives presents to relatives of someone deceased in completion of mourning on anniversary of the death

giiwose *vai* s/he hunts

giizhaa *adv* ahead of time; beforehand; in advance

giizhi- *pv* finish; complete

giizhigad *vii* it is day

giizhigad *ni* day; **ogiizhigadomiwaa** their days

giizhiikan *vti* complete it, finish with it; *reduplicated form* **gaakiizhiikan**

giizhiikigaade *vii* it is finished (by someone); "they" finish it

giizhiitaa *vai* s/he finishes work, s/he finishes a task; *reduplicated form* **gaakiizhiitaa**

giizikan *vti* take it off your body (e.g., clothes)

giizis *na* sun, moon, month

giizisijigaade *vii* it is completely laid out (by someone); "they" completely lay it out

giizizan *vti* cook it

-go *pc* [emphatic word]; *also* **igo**

gomaapii *adv* for sometime, some distance, after a while

goshi /goS-/ *vta* fear h/

goshkwaakoshkan *vti* shake it

goshkwaabaawe *vai* s/he is startled by water being splashed on h/

gotan *vti* be afraid of it, fear it

Gookomisakiinaan *name pers* our grandmother, the Earth (Wenabozho's grandmother); Manidoo

goopadenindizo *vai* s/he considers h/self worthless

goopadizi *vai* s/he is worthless, is inferior

gwayak *adv* straight, right, correct

gwaaba'an *vti* scoop it up, ladle it out

gweki-manidoowi *vai* s/he turns into a Manidoo

gwiinawaabam *vta* fail to see h/

gwiinawaabaminaagozi *vai* s/he is unable to be seen, is no longer seen; *reduplicated form* **gaagwiinawaabaminaagozi**

gwiinawaabandan *vti* fail to see h/

gwiinawendan *vti* miss, feel the absence of it; *reduplicated form* **gaagwiinawendan**

gwiinawenim *vta* miss h/, feel the absence of h/; *reduplicated form* **gaagwiinawenim**

gwiiwizens *na* boy

igo *pc* [emphatic word]; *also* **-go**

i'iw *pron dem* that; *inanimate singular demonstrative*; also **iw**

i'iwapii *adv* at that time

ikido *vai* s/he says, s/he speaks

ikidowin *ni* word, speech

iko *pc* used to, formerly, it was the custom to; *also* **-ko**

ikowebinan *vti* toss it aside, shove it aside, abandon it

ikwe *na* woman

ikwewi *vai* she is female

imaa *adv* there

ina *pc* (yes-no question word); *also* **na**

inabi *vai* s/he sits a certain way, sits there

inagim *vta* set a certain price on h/, designate h/, intend h/ for a certain purpose

ina'igaade *vii* it is sung a certain way, "they" sing it a certain way

ina'oonwewizi *vai* s/he is given things, is gifted a certain way

inakamigizi *vai* s/he does a certain thing, s/he has such happen to h/

inamo *vii* it leads to a certain place (as a road or trail)

inanjige *vai* s/he eats a certain way

inawem *vta* be related to h/

inawemaagan *na* a relative; **gidinawemaaganag** *nid* your relatives; **gidinawemaaganinaan** *nid* our (inclusive) relative; **gidinawemaaganinaanig** *nid* our (inclusive) relatives; **gidinawemaaganiwaa** *nid* your (plural) relative; **indinawemaaganidog** *nid* you my relatives; *vocative plural;* **odinawemaaganan** *nad* h/ relative(s); **odinawemaaganiwaan** *nad* their relative(s)

inawendaaso *vai* s/he is related in a certain way; **zayaagi-inawendaasojig** close relatives

inaabadad *vii* it is useful in a certain way, is employed in a certain way

inaabam *vta* see h/ a certain way as in a dream

inaabaso *vai* h/ smoke goes a certain way

inaabi *vai* s/he looks to a certain place

inaabogo *vai* s/he moves a certain way on the water

inaadizi *vai* s/he has a certain character; s/he has a certain way of life

inaajim *vta* tell of h/ a certain way, narrate of h/ a certain way

inaajimo *vai* s/he tells a certain way, s/he narrates a certain way

inaakonige *vai* s/he decides things a certain way, s/he agrees on something

inaanimad *vii* the wind blows a certain way

inaanzozhe *vai* s/he has skin of a certain color

indawaas *adv* therefore; consequently; rather; might as well

indayi'iiman /-ayi'iim-/ *nid* my clothing (plural)

indede /-dedey-/ *nad* my father

indoodem /-doodem-/ *nad* my totem, my clan

indoozhim /-doozhim-/ *nad* my parallel nephew (male's brother's son or female's sister's son); **odoozhiman** h/ nephew(s)

inendam *vai2* s/he thinks a certain way, decides, agrees

inendamowin *ni* mind, thoughts

inendan *vti* think of it a certain way

inendaagozi *vai* s/he is thought of a certain way, seems to be a certain way, has a certain destiny

inendaagwad *vii* it is thought of a certain way, seems to be a certain way; has a certain destiny

inenim *vta* think of h/ a certain way, meant for h/ a certain way

inenindizo *vai* s/he thinks of h/self a certain way

ingitiziim /-gitiziim-/ *nad* my parent

ingiw *pron dem* those; *animate plural demonstrative*

ingoding *adv* sometime; at one time

ingoji *adv* somewhere, anywhere, approximately, nearly

inigaachigaazo *vai* s/he is abused (by someone); "they" abuse h/

inigaa' *vta* treat h/ badly, abuse h/, hurt h/

inigaawendam *vai* s/he feels bad

inigaazi *vai* s/he is pitiful

inigokwekamig *adv* abundance

inikaa *vai* s/he goes a certain way

inikweshin *vai* s/he lies with h/ head a certain way

ininamaw *vta* hand it to h/ a certain way

inini *na* man

initaagozi *vai* s/he is sounds a certain way

iniw *pron dem* that; *animate obviative demonstrative*; those; *inanimate plural demonstrative; also* **inow**

inow *pron dem* that; *animate obviative demonstrative*; those; *inanimate plural demonstrative; also* **iniw**

inoo'amaw *vta* point to (it) for h/

inootaw *vta* quote h/ a certain way

inwe *vai* s/he speaks a certain language

inwewe *vii* it makes a certain noise

inwewetoo *vai* s/he makes a certain noise, speaks a certain way

inwewin *ni* a language

ipide *vii* it moves speedily a certain way

isa *pc* [emphatic word]; *also* **sa**

ishke *pc* look!, behold!

ishkode *ni* fire

ishkodens *ni* match

ishkonigan *ni* reservation

ishkwaa-ayaa *vai* s/he has passed, is dead

ishkwaakide *vii* it is left behind from fire

ishkwaakizi *vai* s/he is left behind from fire

ishkwaandem *ni* door

ishwaaswi *adv* eight

ishkweyaang *adv* behind; in the past

ishpiming *adv* in the sky, above

iw *pron dem* that; *inanimate singular demonstrative; also* **i'iw**

iwedi *pron dem* that over there; *inanimate singular demonstrative*

iwidi *adv* over there

izhaa *vai* s/he goes to a certain place

izhaamagad *vii* it goes to a certain place

izhi /iN-/ *vta* say to h/, speak so to h/

izhi- *pv* in a certain way, to a certain place, thus, so, there

izhi-ayaa *vai* s/he is a certain way

izhi-wiindan *vti* call it a certain way, name it a certain way

izhi-wiinjigaade *vii* it is named a certain way (by someone); "they" name it a certain way

izhi-wiinzh /izhi-wiin-/ *vta* call h/ a certain way, name h/ a certain way

izhichigaade *vii* it is made a certain way (by someone); "they" make it a certain way

izhichige *vai* s/he does things a certain way

izhigiizhwe *vai* s/he talks a certain way

izhikawe *vai* s/he leaves tracks going to a certain place

izhinan *vti* see it a certain way, perceive it a certain way

izhinaagozi *vai* s/he has a certain appearance, s/he has a certain look

izhinikaadan *vti* name it a certain way

izhinikaazo *vai* s/he is named a certain way

izhinikaazowin *ni* a personal or family name

izhinoo'amaw *vta* point to (it) for h/

izhinoo'an *vti* point to it in a certain way

izhishim *vta* put, lay, set h/ a certain way

izhisin *vii* it lies a certain way; it is performed a certain way

izhitwaawin *ni* custom, cultural or religious belief or practice

izhiwebad *vii* it happens a certain way, it is a certain event, it is a certain weather condition

izhiwebizi *vai* s/he behaves a certain way, s/he has certain things happen to h/, fares a certain way

izhiwidoon *vti* take it to a certain place, carry it to a certain place

izhiwijigaade *vii* it is taken, carried to a certain place (by someone); "they" take, carry it to a certain place

izhizideshin *vai* s/he lies with h/ feet a certain way

jaagide *vii* it burns up

jaagizigaade *vii* it is burned (by someone); "they" burn it

jaagizigaazo *vai* s/he is burned (by someone); "they" burn h/

jiibayi-makak *ni* casket

jiibaakwaadamaw *vta* cook (it) for h/

jiibaakwaan *ni* cooking

jiibaakwe *vai* s/he cooks

jiibewigamig *ni* funeral home

-ko *pc* used to, formerly, it was the custom to; *also* **iko**

madweshim *vta* make h/ sound by dropping or hitting h/, ring h/

makakoons *ni* small box, small birch bark basket

makandamaw *vta* take (it) from h/, deprive h/ (of it)

makizin *ni* moccasin, shoe

mamaajii *vai* s/he moves, s/he is in motion

mami /mam-/ *vta* take h/

mamigaade *vii* it is taken (by someone), "they" take it

mamiikwaam *vta* brag about h/

mamiiziwe *adv* everywhere, all over; *reduplication of* **miziwe**

mamoon *vti2* take it

manaaji' *vta* treat h/ with respect

manaajitoon *vti* treat h/ with respect, handle it carefully

manezi *vai+o* s/he lacks (it)

Manidoo *na* spirit, god, Manidoo; **owiiji-manidooman** the one or ones who are with h/ as Manidoo

Manidoo Naagaanizid *name pers* Leader of the Manidoo; Creator

manidoo-dewe'igan *na* ceremonial drum

manidoo-giigidowin *ni* ceremonial song

manidookaazo *vai* s/he attempts ceremonies, takes on spiritual powers by h/ own authority

manidoons *na* bug, insect

manidoowaadad *vii* it has a spiritual nature

manidoowaadizi *vai* s/he has a spiritual nature

manidoowi *vai* s/he is a spirit, is a Manidoo

manidoowichige *vai* s/he has or participates in a ceremony

manoomin *ni* wild rice

mashkawaa *vii* it is powerful

mashkimod *ni* bag, sack

mashkimodens *ni* small bag, small sack

mawadisan *vti* visit it

mawi *vai* s/he cries, s/he weeps

mawinzo *vai* s/he picks berries

mazinaatese *vii* it is a show

maa *adv* for sometime, some distance; some amount; to a middling degree; also **gomaa**

maada'adoo *vai* s/he goes off following a trail

maada'ookii *vai+o* s/he passes (it) out

maada'oozh /maada'ooN-/ *vta* pass it out to h/

maadaabaso *vai* h/ smoke is going out, starting off

maadaanagidoon *vai* s/he starts off talking

maagizhaa *adv* maybe; I think that... , perhaps

maajaa *vai* s/he leaves, departs, starts off

maajaa' *vta* hold a funeral for h/

maajaa'iwe *vai* s/he holds a funeral, speaks at a funeral

maajaa'iwewin *ni* funeral

maajaamagad *vii* it leaves, departs, starts off

maajitaa *vai* s/he starts an activity

maajiidoon *vti* take it away, take it along

maajiigin *vii* it grows up, starts to grow

maajiikamigaa *vii* it is the future

maamandoogwaason *ni* quilt

maamaw- *pv* most (of all)

maamawi *adv* together

maamawichigewag *vai-pl* they help one another, do things together

maamiginan *vti* pick it up, gather it

maamiijin *vti3* keep eating it; *reduplication of* **miijin**

maamiizh /**maamiiN-**/*vta* give (it) to h/; *reduplication of:* **miizh** /**miiN-**/

maanoo *adv* never mind; let it be; don't bother; don't care

maazhichige *vai* s/he does wrong, does bad things

maazhise *vai* s/he has something bad happen to h/

megwaa *adv* while, as, during (the time)

Memengwesiwag *na-pl* Little People in the Woods; Manidoog; *also* **Manidoo-gwiiwizensag**

Memiigwanaajig *vai (plural participle)* The feathered ones; Birds; Manidoo

memwech *adv* just that, exactly, it is so; **gaawiin memwech** it is not necessary

meshkwadoonigan *na* money

mewinzha *adv* a long time ago, long ago

michisag *ni* floor

midaaso-diba'iganed *vii* it is ten o'clock

mide *na* a member of the Midewiwin

mide-maajaa'iwe *vai* s/he holds a Midewiwin funeral, s/he speaks at a Midewiwin funeral

midewi'iwe *vai* s/he conducts a Midewiwin ceremony for people

mikan *vti* find it

mikwendam *vai2* s/he recollects, remembers, s/he has things come to one's mind

mikwendan *vti* remember it, recollect it, come to think of it

mikwenim *vta* remember h/, recollect h/, come to think of h/

minawaanigozi *vai* s/he is happy, is joyous, has a good time

minawaanigwad *vii* it is happy, is exciting

mindido *vai* s/he is big

mindimooyenh *na* old lady, old woman

minik *adv* a certain amount, a certain number, so much, so many

minikwe *vai+o* s/he drinks (it)

minikwewin *ni* alcohol, drink

minjimin *vta* hold on to h/

minjiminan *vti* hold on to it

minjinawezi *vai* s/he has a difficult time with a loss or from a loss, grieves

mino- *pv* good, nice, well

mino-ayaawin *ni* good health

mino-doodaw *vta* do h/ good, treat h/ well

minochige *vai* s/he does good, does the right thing

minokan *vti* fit it well

minwaabishin *vai* s/he sees something beautiful, likes what h/ sees

minwendam *vai2* s/he is happy

minwendan *vti* like it

minwii *vai* s/he moves easily, works without distraction, is efficient

misabi *vai* s/he kneels down

misawaa *adv* no matter what; even though, even if, despite

misawendam *vai2* s/he desires, wants

misawendamaw *vta* desires (it) from h/

misawendan *vti* desire, want it

Misi-zaaga'igan *name place* Mille Lacs Lake; Mille Lacs reservation

miskobii'igaazo *vai* s/he is painted red (by someone); "they" paint h/ red

miskogoodemagad *vii* is hangs red in color

miskokamigaa *vii* it is red ground

miskomin *na* raspberry

Mitigwaabiiwinini *name pers* The Bow Man; Tree; Manidoo

Mizhakwad *name pers* Albert Churchill

miziwe *adv* all over, everywhere; *reduplicated form* **mamiiziwe**

mii *adv* it is thus that, it is that

miigis *na* Mide shell, pearl

miigwech *pc* thanks!

miigwechiwi' *vta* thank h/

miigwechiwitaagozi *vai* s/he gives thanks

miijin *vti3* eat it; *reduplicated form* **maamiijin**

miikanens *ni* path, road

miinan /**miin-**/ *ni-pl* blueberries

miinawaa *adv* again, and, also

miinigoowizi *vai* s/he is given (in a spiritual way)

miizh /miin-/ *vta* give (it) to h/; *reduplicated form* **maamiizh** /maamiiN-/

mookinigaade *vii* it is revealed(by someone), "they" reveal it

mookii *vai* s/he emerges, comes out

mookomaan *ni* knife

mookomaanens *ni* little knife

moonendan *vti* realize, sense it

moonenim *vta* sense h/

moozhag *adv* often, constantly, several times

moozhi' *vta* feel h/ in or on your body

moozhitoon *vti2* feel it in or on your body

nabagisag *na* board

Nabaanaabe *na* Mermaid; Manidoo

nagadan *vti* abandon it

nagadenim *vta* form a relationship with h/, be acquainted with h/

nagamo *vai* s/he sings

nagamon *ni* song

nagazh /nagaN-/ *vta* leave h/ behind

nagishkaw *vta* meet h/ (while going somewhere)

na'in *vta* bury h/, put h/ away, store h/

na'inigaazo *vai* s/he is put away (by someone); "they" put h/ away; s/he is buried; *reduplication* **nanaa'inigaazo**

nakom *vta* answer h/ (in agreement), agree with h/; *reduplicated form* **nanaakom**

nakwetan *vti* answer it (in agreement), agree and accept it

namanjinik *ni* left hand

nanaa'inigaazo *vai* s/he is put away (by someone); "they" put h/ away; s/he is buried; *reduplication of* **na'inigaazo**

nanaa'isidoon *vti2* correct it, adjust it, change it

nanaamadabi *vai* s/he sits, sits down

nanaandawi'iwe *vai* s/he heals people, doctors people

nanaandom *vta* ask for, call, summon h/

nandodamaw *vta* ask h/ for (it), beg h/ for (it)

nandodan *vta* ask for, call, summon h/

naniizaanichige *vai* s/he does dangerous things

napaaj *adv* opposite

nasanaamo *vai* s/he releases h/ emotions

nawagikwebi *vai* s/he sits with h/ head down

nawaj *adv* more

nawajii *vai* s/he takes a lunch break

nawajii' *vta* feed h/ lunch

nawapwaan *ni* lunch taken along

Nazhike-awaasang *name pers* The Star That Shines Alone (Evening Star); Manidoo

Nazhike-awaasang *name pers* Mary Churchill-Benjamin

Nazhikewigaabawiikwe *name pers* Sophia Churchill-Benjamin

naa *adv* again, and, also; *also* **miinawaa**

naa *pc* [emphatic word]

naabikawaagan *ni* necktie, necklace

naabishkaage *vai* s/he accepts or takes something for someone, partakes in an offering on someone else's behalf

naadamaw *vta* help h/

naadamaage *vai* s/he helps people

naadamaagoowizi *vai* s/he is helped (in a spiritual way)

naadin *vti3* go get it, fetch it, go after it

naanaadamaadiwag /naanaadamaadi-/ *vai* they help each other

naangitaa *vai* s/he is lightweight

naaniigaan *adv* ahead, leading, at the front

naaniigaaniimagad *vii* it goes ahead, leads

naano-biboon *adv* five years

naawayi'ii *adv* in the middle

naaweweshin *vai* s/he is heard off in the distance

Naawi-giizhik *na* Center of the Sky; Manidoo

naazhaabaawemagad *vii* it washes downward

naazikan *vti* go to it, approach it

naazikaw *vta* go to h/, approach h/

naazikaage *vai* s/he goes to people, approaches people

nebowa *adv* many, much; a lot

ni- *pv* going away, going along, in progress, on the way, coming up in time; *also* **ani-**

nibi *ni* water

nibiikaang *adv* in the water

nigaapoono *vai+o* s/he eats (berries)

nimaamaa /-maamaa(y)-/ *nad* my mother

nimishoome /-mishoomey-/ *nad* my parallel uncle

nindede /-dede(y)-/ *nid* my father

ningaabii'an *ni* west; **ningaabii'anong** in the west

ningwa'igaazo *vai* s/he is buried

niningwanis /-ningwanis-/ *nad* my cross-nephew (male's sister's son or female's brother's son)

nininj /-ninjy-/ *nid* my hand, my finger

niniijaanis /-niijaanis-/ *nad* my child

ninoshenh /-nosheny-/ *nad* my parallel aunt (mother's sister)

nisayenh /-sayeny-/ *nad* my older brother, my older male parallel cousin

nishi /niS-/ *vta* kill h/

nishiime /-shiimey-/ *nad* my younger sibling (brother or sister)

nishkiinzhig /-shkiinzhigw-/ *nid* my eye

nishwanaaji' *vta* destroy h/, mess h/ up

nising *adv* three times

niswi *adv* three

nitam *adv* first

nitaa- *pv* know how to do something; be good at; be skilled at; frequently do

nitaawigi' *vta* grow h/, raise h/

niwiijikiwenh /-iijikiweny-/ *nad* my (male's) brother

niwiiw /-wiiw-/ *nad* my wife

nizhishenh /-zhisheny-/ *nad* my cross-uncle (mother's brother)

nizid /-zid-/ *nid* my foot

nizigos /-zigos-/ *nad* my cross-aunt (father's sister)

niibawi *vai* s/he stands

Niibaa-giizhik *name pers* Archie Mosay

niigaan *adv* ahead, leading, at the front; in the future

niigaanizh /niigaaniN-/ *vta* put h/ first

niigaanizi *vai* s/he is the leader

niigaanii *vai* s/he goes ahead, leads

niimi *vai* s/he dances

niin *pron per* I, me; *first person singular pronoun*

niindaa' *vta* send (it) to h/

niindaa'iwe *vai* s/he sends (it) to people

niisaakiiwemagad *vii* it goes downhill

niiwin *adv* four

niiwing *adv* four times

niiyaw /-iiyaw-/ *nad* my body

niiyo-dibik *adv* four nights

niiyo-giizhigad *vii* it is the fourth day

niiyo-giizhik *adv* four days

niizh *adv* two

niizhing *adv* two times

niizhiwag /niizhi-/ *vai* they are two, there are two of them

niizhosagoons *adv* two thousand

noogigaabawi *vai* s/he stops and stands in a place

noogitaa *vai* s/he stops an activity, stops working

nookomis /-ookomis-/ *nad* my grandmother

noomage- *pv* completely

noomaya *adv* recently; a while ago; a little while ago

noondan *vti* hear it

noondaw *vta* hear h/

noondaagozi *vai* s/he can be heard (by someone), "you" can hear h/

noongom *adv* now, nowadays, today

Obizaan *name pers* Lee Staples

odaabaan *na* car

odaapin *vta* accept (it) from h/, take h/

odaapinan *vti* accept it, take it

odedeyiwi *vai+o* s/he has h/ as h/ father

ode'imin *ni* strawberry

odish /odiS-/ *vta* come upon h/, visit h/, meet up with h/

oditan *vti* come upon it

odoodeman /-doodem-/ *nad* h/ clan

odoozhiman /-doozhim-/ *nad* h/ parallel nephew(s) (male's brother's son or female's sister's son)

ogidaakiiwemagad *vii* It goes uphill

ogijayi'ii *adv* on top of it

Ogimaawab *name pers* John Benjamin

ogookomisan /-gookomis-/ *nad* h/ grandmother

o'ow *pron dem* this; *inanimate singular demonstrative*

o'owapii *adv* at this time

ojibwemo *vai* s/he speaks Ojibwe

ojibwemotaw *vta* speak Ojibwe to h/

ojibwemowin *ni* Ojibwe language

ojichaagwan /-jichaagw-/ *nad* h/ spirit

ojijiingwanabi *vai* s/he squats

ojijiingwanigaabawi *vai* s/he bends over

okaad /-kaad-/ *nid* his leg

okobii'igaazo *vai* s/he is written in a list (by someone); "they" are written in a list

okwi'idiwag /okwi'idi-/ *vai* they get together

omaa *adv* here

omaamaayiwi *vai+o* s/he has her as h/ mother

ombi' *vta* excite h/, motivate h/

Ombishkebines *names pers* Chato Gonzalez

omoodens *ni* little bottle, vase

onaabam *vta* select h/

onaagan *ni* dish, plate

onaagoshin /**onaagoshi-**/ *vii* it is evening; **endaso-onaagoshig** every evening

onaajiwan *vii* it is beautiful

ondanjige *vai* s/he eats in a certain place

ondinan *vti* get it from a certain place, obtain it from a certain place

ondinige *vai* s/he gets things from a certain place, obtains something from a certain place

oninj /**-ninjy-**/ *nid* h/ hand

onishkaa *vai* s/he gets up (from a prone position)

oniigaaniim /**-niigaaniim-**/ *nid* h/ future; **oniigaaniiming** in h/ future; **oniigaaniimiwaang** in their future

oniijaanisan /**-niijaanis-**/ *nad* h/ child or children

onji- *pv* from a certain place, for a certain reason; because

onjibaa *vai* s/he comes from a certain place

onjida *adv* for a reason, on purpose

onjikaa *vai* s/he comes from a certain place

onjikaamagad *vii* it comes from a certain place

onjii *vai* s/he comes from a certain place

onzaam *adv* too (much), excessively, extremely; because

onzaamiikan *vti* overwork it, overdo it

oshkaabewis *na* helper (in a ceremony)

oshki- *pv* new, young, fresh, for the first time

oshki-manoomin *ni* fresh rice

oshkiinzhigokaanan *ni* eyeglasses

owapii *adv* at this time, then

owiiyaw /**-wiiyaw-**/ *nid* h/ body

ozaawaabii'igaazo *vai* s/he is painted with a yellow strip (by someone); "they" paint h/ with a yellow strip

ozhaawashkokamigaa *vii* it is blue ground

ozhaawashkonaanzo *vai* s/he is blue in color

ozhibii'an *vti* write it, write it down

ozhibii'igan *ni* something written, a piece of writing

ozhibii'igaade *vii* it is written (by someone), "they" write it; it is written down (by someone), "they" write it down

ozhibii'igaazo *vai* s/he is written down (as on a list) (by someone), "they" write h/ down

ozhitoon *vti2* make it, build it, create it

ozhishim *vta* lay h/ out

ozhiitaa *vai* s/he gets ready, prepares

ozhiitaa' *vta* prepare h/, get h/ ready

ozid /-zid-/ *nid* h/ foot

ozisidamaw *vta* arrange (it) for h/, put (it) in place for h/

oodena *ni* town

oodetoo *vai* s/he has a community or town

-sa *pc* [emphatic word]; *also* **isa**

sanaa *pc*

wa'aw *pron dem* this; *animate singular demonstrative*

wanendan *vti* forget it

wanenim *vta* forget h/

waniba' *vta [in inverse form]* it eludes h/

wanibii'ige *vai* s/he makes a mistake in writing

wani' *vta* lose h/

wanishkwebidoon *vti2* distract it, interrupt it, disturb it

wanishkwe' *vta* distract h/, interrupt h/

wanitaaso *vai* s/he loses someone

waniwebinige *vai* s/he speaks incorrectly, does something incorrect

waniike *vai+o* forget (it)

wasidaawendam *vai2* s/he is sad, sorrowful, grieving

wasidaawendamowin *ni* grief

wawaaj *adv* and even

wawaanim *vta* stump h/ (by speech)

wawiinge *adv* properly; carefully; completely; well

wawiinge'oonwewizi *vai* s/he is completely given

wawiingezi *vai* s/he is efiicient, is thorough

wayaabishkiiwe *na* white man; *see also* **waabishkiiwe** *vai*

wayeshkad *adv* at first; in the beginning

wayezhim *vta* cheat h/

waabam *vta* see h/; *reduplicated form* **waawaabam**

waabanda'iwe *vai* s/he shows something to people

waabandan *vti* see it

waabanoke *vai* s/he is in the process of tomorrow, does tomorrow

waabanong *adv* in the east; to the east

waabashkiki *ni* swamp

waabigwaniins *ni* flower

waabishkiiwe *vai* s/he is a white person

waabooyaan *ni* blanket

waabooz *na* rabbit

waakaabiwag /waakaabi-/ *vai* they sit around in circle

waakaa'igan *ni* house, building

waasa *adv* far, far away distant

waasechigan *ni* window

Waasigwan *name pers* [in this book **Waasigwan** stands for the name of the deceased person]

waawaabam *vta* see h/; *reduplication of* **waabam**

waawaashkeshi *na* deer

waawaateshkaa *vii* it is bright and shiny in color

waawiindamaw *vta* explain to h/, tell about it to h/, promise it to h/

waawiindamaage *vai* s/he explains about (it) to people

waawiindamaagoowizi *vai* s/he is explained to, is told (in a spiritual way)

Wenabozho *name pers* the Manidoo who once lived among us as a man

wenda- *pv* really; completely; just so; especially

wenipanad *vii* it is easy, it is cheap

wenjida *adv* especially

wenjise *vai* s/he gets by cheap, gets things cheaply

weweni *adv* in a good way, properly, correctly, carefully, safely

wewiib *adv* hurry, in a hurry, quickly

wii- *pv* is going to, want to, will

wiidanokiim *vta* work with h/

wiidoopam *vta* eat with h/, share food with h/

wiigiwaam *ni* wigwam

wiigwaas *ni* birch bark

wiij'ayaaw *vta* be with h/, live or stay with h/

wiij'ayaawaagan *na* someone you live with

wiiji- *pv* with; in company with; one's fellow; **owiiji-anishinaabemiwaan** their fellow Anishinaabe; **giwiiji-bimaadiziiminaan** our fellow human being; **owiiji-manidooman** the one or ones who are with h/ as Manidoo

wiijiiw *vta* go with h/, accompany h/

wiikwajitoon *vti2* try to do it, make an effort to do it

wiin *pc* [contrastive word]

wiin *pron per* he, she; her, him; *third person singular pronoun*

wiinawaa *pron per* they, them; *third person plural personal pronoun*

wiindamaw *vta* tell h/ about (it)

wiindamaage *vai* s/he tells about (it) to people, explains (it) to people

wiindan *vti* name it, mention the name of it

wiinjigaade *vii* it is named (by someone); "they" name it

wiinjigaazo *vai* s/he is named or called (by someone); "they" name or call h/

wiinzh /wiinN-/ *vta* name h/, mention the name of h/, give h/ a name

wiisini *vai* s/he eats

wiisiniwin *ni* food

wiiyagasenh *ni* dust, dirt

zagaswe'idiwag /zagaswe'idi-/ *vai* they have a feast or ceremony

zakab *adv* at peace, quiet

zanagad *vii* it is difficult, it is hard to manage

zazaagitoon *vti2* be stingy with it

zaaga'igan *ni* lake

zaagakii *vii* it sprouts

zaagewe *vai* s/he comes suddenly into view (as from around the corner)

zaagi-dakokii *vai* s/he steps through

zaagi-inawendaaso *vai* s/he is closely related; **zayaagi-inawendaasojig** close relatives

zaagi-maajaa'iwe *vai* s/he holds a Midewiwin funeral for someone who was not a Mide

zaagidin *vta* put h/ out, take h/ out

zaagi' *vta* love h/, treasure h/

zaagi'idizo *vai* s/he has love for h/self

zaagitoon *vti2* love it, treasure it

zegaabaawe *vai* s/he is shocked by a splash of water

zeginaagozi *vai* s/he looks ferocious

zhakamoozh /zhakamooN-/ *vta* spoon-feed h/

zhawendaagozi *vai* s/he is shown compassion, is pitied (by someone), "they" show compassion to, pity h/

zhawenim *vta* have compassion for h/, pity h/

zhawenimitaw *vta* listen to h/ with compassion

zhawenindiwag /zhawenindi-/ *vai* they have compassion for one another

zhazhiibitam *vai2* s/he is stubborn, is disobedient

zhaawanong *adv* in, to, from the south

zhingishin *vai* s/he is lying down

zhiishiigwan *na* rattle

zhoomiingwetaw *vta* smile at h/

zhooniyaa *na* money

ziibi *ni* river

zoongi-midekwewi *vai* she is a fourth degree Mide

Printed in the USA
CPSIA information can be obtained
at www.ICGtesting.com
JSHW022131101223
53530JS00001B/1